Closure

A CONTEMPORARY DRAMA
IN TWO ACTS

by Ron Blicq

A SAMUEL FRENCH ACTING EDITION

SAMUEL FRENCH

FOUNDED 1830

NEW YORK HOLLYWOOD LONDON TORONTO

SAMUELFRENCH.COM

IMPORTANT BILLING AND CREDIT REQUIREMENTS

ABOUT THE AUTHOR

Ron Blicq has been a writer and teacher of business and technical writing for over 30 years. He has authored several textbooks on how to write well, two novels, a biographical description of the evacuation of children from the Channel Islands in 1940, and has scripted and directed six dramatized educational video programs. He has been writing stage plays since 1999, eight of which have been produced and four have won awards.

The inaugural production of **CLOSURE** was presented by GADOC (the Guernsey Amateur Dramatic and Operatic Club) at the Beau Sejour Centre in Guernsey, UK, 25 to 28 October 2005, with the following cast:

DONALD BARLOW . . . . Dennis Burns

DAPHNE BARLOW . . . . Caron Parker

CLAIRE SUMMERS . . . . Nicola Reoch-Brehaut

GORDIE SUMMERS . . . . Alexander Crossan

GORDON DEVEREAUX . . . . John Gaisford

HELEN DEVEREAUX . . . . Jane Blower

PAUL HOOGSTRA . . . . Steven Molnar

The production was directed by Clare Milner.

The author can provide a DVD of the initial production, a source for Squadron Leader Devereaux's uniform, and personal advice for staging the "imaginary flying" sequence.

CHARACTERS

IN THE UK:

DONALD BARLOW – Donald is 54 and is manager of a major bank in Nottingham, England. He is very competent, very knowledgeable, and very good at his work. He is happily married to Daphne, and they have two children: Claire and Kevin; we meet only Claire. They also have one grandchild: Gordie, who is Claire's son, and a major character in the play.

Although a competent decision-maker at work, he prefers to defer to Daphne when decisions are needed at home. He is an easygoing man who seems to have everything going for him, but nevertheless feels there is a 'hole' in his life; that something is missing. He has never known his father, other than being told his father's first name.

His mother (Wendy Barlow) died 12 months before the play opens. Donald was born as the result of a love affair she had with a Canadian flyer, but who disappeared from her life immediately after the war and without knowing she was pregnant. She never married, and worked two jobs to ensure her son received a good education. She was 18 in 1945. Donald was born in February 1946.

DAPHNE BARLOW – Daphne is 51 and is rather conscious of her and Donald's social position (he isn't concerned, but phlegmatically let's her be that way). She loves her husband in a somewhat abstracted but protective way. Her children grew to resent her over-protectiveness, so moved out earlier than they might have done. She trained to be an accountant (she and Donald met at the bank), but on marriage chose to remain at home and bring up her children. Since they left, she has joined a church community group, which she now runs because she is a good organizer and other members let her do it. Her tendency to be outspoken, and to correct speakers if they make a language error, sometimes disturbs people.

CLAIRE SUMMERS – Claire is 28. She has graduated with a degree in journalism and is now a research writer for *The Source*, a middle-road magazine that prints high-quality human-interest stories. She is very good at her work and is well respected in the journalism field.

She is strong-willed, sometimes rash. She loves her father, but only 'likes' her mother (she resents how her mother controls her father and has controlled her and her brother).

When engaged on a project, she is strongly dedicated, self-driven and objective-seeking (a trait her son has inherited from her). This sometimes causes her to be rather brusque when dealing with people – a trait she recognizes and so takes care to "work" her interviews and the people she is interviewing.

She adores her son and is not in any way using him to make a connection with Gordon Devereaux. She talks to him as if he's an adult (she has never used baby language with him) and encourages him in his endeavours, even pushing him beyond his age.

She is married to Malcom, a laid-back individual who is seldom home (during the time period of the play he is in Africa). She recognizes now that the marriage was a mistake and will sue for divorce when he is next in the UK.

GORDIE SUMMERS – Gordie is an active, well-spoken nine-year-old; articulate, very friendly, likeable, and approachable. Some people might think he is precocious, but his forwardness is a natural interest rather than being pushy. He speaks and thinks beyond his years. He knows nothing about his great-grandfather and the connection his grandfather is trying to make.

Gordie admires his grandfather (Donald), likes to talk sports with him—they occasionally go to a soccer match together—but doesn't do other things with him. His grandmother (Daphne) tends to relate more to him and caters to his exploratory mind. When something interests him, he is unshakably goal-oriented.

IN CANADA:

GORDON DEVEREAUX – Gordon is the most complex character in the play. He is now 75, having joined the Royal Canadian Air Force at age 18 (1942). He trained as a pilot and flew deHavilland Mosquito aircraft, first as a low-level intruder and later as a Bomber Command Pathfinder, dropping flares over target areas to guide the bombers flying far above. In late 1944 he led a special raid on a castle near Bruges, to release special prisoners. During the war he saw the devastation, pain and death caused by German bombing in Britain, and then experienced real concern over the damage and death he was causing to the people in German towns. After the war he "closed the book" on his wartime flying and never discussed it with anyone, not even his wife and their two daughters.

After the war he attended the University of British Columbia and obtained a degree in Forestry. He then entered the family lumber and forestry farming business, and eventually became Owner and Director. He ran the business well, and has a natural ability to manage a company and see the direction in which it should be going. He is also accustomed to having his own way and tends to be irascible when challenged or his efforts are thwarted. He is highly respected in the Vancouver social community, and is Commodore of the distinguished Horseshoe Bay Yacht Club.

He and his wife Helen have a comfortable home in North Vancouver. They have two daughters who now live in the US, and two granddaughters, also in the US.

HELEN DEVEREAUX – Now 71, Helen once was a beautiful woman and still carries her age well. She came from a well-to-do family and was the eldest daughter. She has inherited her family's feeling for stability and prominence in the community. She and Gordon have had a successful marriage and enjoy a now-distant but good relationship with their two daughters.

Helen has a hobby – she runs a successful fashion boutique in West Vancouver, but is seldom seen in the shop, preferring to do the buying and be a "silent partner." She also is active with Oxfam. She is a good decision-maker, with good reason: she thinks through a problem thoroughly and makes a decision before taking action or speaking her thoughts.

THE AGENCY INVESTIGATOR:

PAUL HOOGSTRA – Although 47-year-old Paul Hoogstra is essentially a businessperson, he does not have the strong, objective drive of the true entrepreneur. He likes people, likes helping them, and likes what he has to do. He does not, however, enjoy making the contacts with the fathers in Canada, whom he finds to be brutally against what he is trying to achieve.

RECORDED VOICE OVER – Radio announcer plus a male and a female interviewee.

BACKGROUND

Gordon Devereaux was one of 25,000 World War II Canadian service-men whose liaison with a British girl conceived a child, but he returned to Canada at the end of the war unaware that he had done so. He has built up a successful lumber business in western Canada and now, at age 75, is enjoying his retirement with his wife Helen.

Donald Barlow's mother endured considerable financial difficulty, yet managed to send her son to grammar school. He is now manager of a major bank in Nottingham and is married to Daphne. They have two children, but we meet only their daughter Claire and her nine-year-old son Gordie. Barlow's mother died a year before the play opens.

RATIONALE

The idea for the play evolved in the fall of 2002, when I heard reports on the BBC and CBC of sons and daughters in the UK and The Netherlands trying to find their fathers and, in most cases, meeting with absolute refusal and experiencing severe disappointment. I worked fast, because the play needs to appear while the topic and interest are current.

It makes compelling drama because many people today, whether adopted or brought up by a single parent without knowledge of the other parent, are attempting to fill a 'hole' in their lives and so achieve closure.

Ron Blicq
November 2008

THE SET

The action takes place in the living rooms of two homes, one in Nottingham, England, and the other in North Vancouver, Canada. There also are brief scenes in a corner of a motel bedroom in Vancouver (used concurrently with the Nottingham room). The set can be either fixed, as described below, or changed – if facilities permit – by placing the two living rooms back-to-back on a rotating platform. If the stage demands a permanent set and has limited fly space, the following works well.

- Stage left: The Barlow living room in Nottingham, furnished comfortably in a British 1970's mode with some modern additions. Upstage, a window onto the front garden. Stage right, a door to the remainder of the house.
- Stage right: The Devereaux living room in North Vancouver. Upstage centre, a French window overlooking the garden. Upstage left, a door entering the dining room and kitchen area. Downstage left, a door opening onto the front hall. It has high quality modern furniture and wall hangings.
- Above stage level: Above the upstage wall of the Nottingham living room, centre stage and abutting the edge of the Vancouver room, a corner of a motel bedroom with a single bed, a chair and a side table with lamp and telephone. (Alternatively, this set can be built on a roll-on platform.)

MULTIMEDIA

Sound: Two Rolls Royce Merlin aircraft engines, running simultaneously and at various pitches to denote climbing, level flight, and descending; guns firing; bombs bursting.

ACT 1

(The curtain rises on the Barlow residence in Nottingham, England; it is evening, November 2000, dark outside the windows. **DONALD** *is alone, speaking into a mobile phone; he has a posthumous letter from his mother [Wendy] in his hand. He walks about as he talks.)*

DONALD. I don't see how you can be so damned dogmatic, without first seeing...*(listens)* Kevin...Kevin!...Look. My mother – your grandmother – wrote this letter before she died *(waves it as though Kevin can see it)*, so we could all learn more about your grandfather...No, I'm not prepared to read it to you over the phone. This is a family meeting and you should be here...What do you mean, you have to work? This is Saturday night, for Christ's sake...A computer virus?...You have to fix it?...

(Enter **DAPHNE** *and* **CLAIRE**. *They look questioningly at him and he mouths 'Kevin' silently; both raise their eyebrows understandingly.)*

CLAIRE. Typical Kevin!

DONALD. What do you mean: 'Let sleeping dogs lie'? I don't appreciate that one bit....So, that's your opinion... Okay...all right, you've got to go. Goodbye. *(switches off phone, places it on side table; to* **CLAIRE***)* That brother of yours! *(to them both)* I chose Saturday night so we could all be here.

DAPHNE. Don't get so worked up, Don. You know what Kevin's like.

CLAIRE. He knows just how to push your buttons!

DONALD. It wouldn't have taken much, to drive up from Bracknell.

DAPHNE. *(to* **CLAIRE***)* It would be nice to see him, just once in a while.

DONALD. *(to* **CLAIRE***)* Where's Gordie? Didn't you bring him with you?

CLAIRE. Having a sleep-over with David Bradley. I don't have to rush back.

DAPHNE. Claire's staying the night.

DONALD. All the more reason to bring Gordie.

DAPHNE. Not the right night, Don. When we have to discuss...your idea...

DONALD. Right...

DAPHNE. *(to* **CLAIRE***)* Much as we like to see him.

DONALD. Right.

CLAIRE. Nice for me, though. I can sleep in.

DONALD. *(an arm around her shoulder)* And you can have our sole attention!

    *(***CLAIRE** *laughs.)*

    (points to liquor on side table) What's your poison tonight? You don't have to drive.

CLAIRE. Still have that Glen Morangie?

DONALD. *(holds up bottle)* A new one. Daphne found it.

DAPHNE. I remembered, from your Dad's birthday.

DONALD. No ice. Water on the side. Right? *(***CLAIRE** *nods.)* Daphne?

DAPHNE. Sherry, I think. Bristol Cream, if we have it.

DONALD. We do. *(to* **CLAIRE***)* Are you still working on that mad cow story? Impact on farmers? Was the massive slaughter necessary?

CLAIRE. No. It's gone to press. On the shelves first of December.

DONALD. Are you happy with it?

CLAIRE. Yes. For once! I just hope it has the right impact.

DONALD. What are you working on now, then?

CLAIRE. A bit hush-hush. Can't say much yet.

DAPHNE. Not even to us? Surely?

CLAIRE. Let's say it's got political overtones. All right?

    (slight pause)

DONALD. Any word from Malcom?

CLAIRE. Still in South Africa. Working as a safari guide, the last I heard.

DAPHNE. You can't start divorce proceedings if he's not here to defend...

CLAIRE. Being separated's fine, Mum, for the moment. Less costly. Less hassle. *(holds up glass)* Cheers!

(DONALD *and* DAPHNE *respond. They are all seated. Slight pause.)*

So, what's up, Dad?

DONALD. Well, I've been sort of playing with an idea...

DAPHNE. *(interrupts; deprecatory)* He wants to trace his father.

DONALD. *(annoyed at her intervention; this is his undertaking)* Daphne!

CLAIRE. Why now, Dad? You've never taken any interest before.

DONALD. Not entirely true.

DAPHNE. Well, you haven't!

DONALD. I never had enough information before. Just a first name: Gordon.

CLAIRE. But now you have?

DAPHNE. He only thinks he has.

DONALD. When I was sorting through your grandmother's papers... *(slight pause)*

CLAIRE. *Your* mother? Wendy?

DONALD. *(nods)* I found an envelope, sealed, with this letter in it.

CLAIRE. She wrote it just before she died? Like, sort of, a last word?

DONALD. Frankly, I don't know. Could have been some time before.

CLAIRE. The paper's a bit yellow: looks aged.

DAPHNE. I don't understand why she didn't just tell you herself, while she was alive.

CLAIRE. *(glances with irritation at* **DAPHNE***)* What does she say, Dad?

DONALD. Not much, really. *(opens letter, reads)* "My dear son. I have never told you much about your father, mostly because there has not been much to tell. He was a pilot in the air force; you knew that. And his name was Gordon; you knew that too. He used to fly out of Scampton aerodrome for a while, near Lincoln. Then he was moved away, to somewhere in Norfolk, I think. But not so far he couldn't come back to visit when he had a forty-eight-hour pass. But there were two things I did not tell you: he was a Canadian and his surname was Devereaux." *(spells it out)* D - e - v - e - r - e - a - u - x.

CLAIRE. You never asked what his surname was?

DONALD. Oh, yes, I did. But her answer was always the same: "Your name is Donald Gordon Barlow, and you should be proud of it."

DAPHNE. Exactly! Just like her.

CLAIRE. So you didn't know he was Canadian?

DONALD. No. I always thought he was R.A.F. When I was young I used to invent stories about him: that he lived in Wales – or Scotland – or was from a well-known family – a titled family; or was already married and my mother chose not to say anything to protect his identity.

CLAIRE. Was it just a passing phase for Gran? Or more than that?

DONALD. Much more, I think. I didn't notice at first, but as I grew older I began to realize…*(sad; slight pause)* It was *how* she spoke of him. *(to* **DAPHNE***, reaching a hand toward her)* Like how we speak to each other.

*(*DAPHNE *reaches up, touches his hand.)*

CLAIRE. She never tried to find him?

DONALD. Not that I am aware of. Actually, I think she thought he died in the war. Right at the end, in the fight against Japan. *(reads)* "I only ever had one letter from him, and it was a postcard, just before the air force sent him to the Pacific. Now I want you to have it."

(He lifts out a black-and-white picture postcard, goes to hand it to **CLAIRE**, *then changes his mind and passes it to* **DAPHNE**. *She turns it over, looks at photograph.)*

DAPHNE. Bournemouth Pier. Pre-war. Doesn't look like that now.

DONALD. Canadian flyers were billeted in Bournemouth during the war. It was a staging post. I found out that much.

CLAIRE. Mum! What does it *say?*

DAPHNE. *(reads)* "Miss Wendy Barlow, 28 Shelford Road, Lincoln. Twenty-third of May, 1945. *(slight pause)* My Dear Wendy:

*(**CLAIRE***'s hand jumps to her throat.)*

I have to tell you that I'm on the move again: help finish the war with Japan. I'll write when I get there, as soon as I can. Take care. Stay young and beautiful. Love, Gordon." *(to* **DONALD***)* And she never heard from him again?

DONALD. Apparently not.

CLAIRE. *(wistfully)* It's like finding a secret compartment in a jewelry box.

DONALD. I know.

DAPHNE. When did the Pacific War end?

DONALD. About three months later: August. After the Yanks dropped the atom bomb. Hiroshima; Nagasaki.

DAPHNE. So there was time, for him still to fly…when he was there?

DONALD. Presumably.

CLAIRE. When did the European war end?

DAPHNE. Eighth of May, 1945.

DONALD. V.E. Day. Victory Europe.

CLAIRE. *(thoughtfully – she's making a calculation on her fingers)* Dad!…Dad?…You're a Victory Day baby!

DONALD. *(not understanding)* I don't quite…

CLAIRE. Your birthday's seventh February. Right?

DONALD. Nineteen-forty-six.

CLAIRE. That's *exactly* nine months after V.E. day!

DAPHNE. Oh, Claire! How could you be so vulgar?!

DONALD. *(laughs)* Well I'll be damned. *(shakes head)* I never realized…*(trails off)*

DAPHNE. Oh, Don! Finish the letter.

DONALD. Oh, yes. *(reads)* "He was a fine man, Donald. He would have been so proud of you. And you of him. I wish life had been different, and you could have known each other. *(slight pause)* With much love, Mum."

CLAIRE. Oh, Dad. *(almost in tears; rises quickly, stands behind his chair, puts her hands on his shoulders, brushes her cheek across the top of his head)* It's so sad. Heartbreaking.

DONALD. I feel as if she's saying: "See if you can find him."

DAPHNE. Don't, Don. Come down to earth. Be realistic.

CLAIRE. *(gives* DAPHNE *a deprecatory glance)* Dad! It's so… *(shrugs)* romantic.

DONALD. There's a postscript: "P.S. Gordon used to say he could see mountains from his bedroom window, with snow on them."

CLAIRE. She's giving you a clue! Like she's *inviting* you to search for him.

DAPHNE. Your father has much better things to do than…

CLAIRE. *(interrupts)* Mother! It's for *Dad* to decide!

(painful pause)

DONALD. No, Claire. Not really. It has to be a family decision. That's why I wanted you and Kevin here, tonight.

CLAIRE. Humph! Kevin will be against it.

DAPHNE. Don't jump to conclusions.

CLAIRE. Automatically.

DONALD. Give him time. He hasn't seen this yet *(holds up letter).*

*(*DAPHNE *holds up her sherry glass.)*

Right! Claire?

CLAIRE. No thanks. I'm fine.

(**DONALD** *collects* **DAPHNE**'s *glass, pours a drink, returns it.*)

DAPHNE. *(reaches for letter; holds it up)* Probably French. Look at his name: Devereaux. Half the population of Canada's French.

CLAIRE. No, Mum. More like twenty percent.

DAPHNE. There'll be Devereauxs all over the place.

CLAIRE. Oh, Mother! Do you have to be so…negative?

DAPHNE. *(to* **DONALD***)* How do you know he's alive, even? Maybe he did die near the end of the war. That would explain why Wendy never heard from him. I mean, I doubt he told his family about her. They wouldn't know it would be…appropriate…to contact her, to tell her.

DONALD. True. There's really very little information to go on.

DAPHNE. Even if they did, would they have bothered?

CLAIRE. Mother! You're so cynical!

DAPHNE. You've got to be realistic, Claire. *(to* **DONALD***)* Don, why do you want to do this?

CLAIRE. Wouldn't you, if it was your…?

DAPHNE. *(interrupts)* I asked your father!

DONALD. It's difficult to explain. I'd not thought about it really. No, that's not true: I *had* thought about it, but only in vague terms. Sort of: 'How nice it would be.' When I was at grammar school, often I was the only boy in my class who didn't have both a mother and a father.

CLAIRE. Hardly the same today. Gordie's one of nine single-parent children in a class of twenty-three.

DAPHNE. But you're not a single parent, dear.

CLAIRE. Might as well be. Malcom's never here. Just a matter of time: when I can pin him down long enough to serve papers. Whatever.

DONALD. I always felt sort of…different: apart from the other boys. Incomplete. Must be hard for you to see: you've always known what it's like to grow up in a complete family. I never have.

CLAIRE. Not so rare today.

DONALD. Not the same.

(Pause; they look questioningly at him.)

They know who their father is.

DAPHNE. Or their mother.

DONALD. Not often.

DAPHNE. Give credit where it's due.

CLAIRE. There was one in Gordie's class, last year. Barnaby. His mother died; cancer, I think. Not sure how his dad coped. They moved away.

DONALD. It's better when a parent dies.

DAPHNE. How can you say that!

DONALD. Think about it…If a father or mother dies, the children know that parent didn't just *choose* to walk out on them.

CLAIRE. Kids often think they're to blame: the parent leaves because of something they did.

DAPHNE. How do you know?

CLAIRE. Research. A story I've been writing.

DAPHNE. Will Gordie feel…? *(pauses)*

CLAIRE. No. I doubt it. He's so accustomed to Malcolm not being here; travelling. *(to* **DONALD***)* Did you think you were to blame?

DONALD. No. Never. Mother made it quite clear: he died, or he just didn't know about me.

CLAIRE. Was that easier for you?

DONALD. In a way. Helped me understand better. *(slight pause)* Yet I still missed having a dad to kick a football around; or take me fishing; repair a puncture on my bike; just to talk to. *(slight pause)*. My mother knew; tried so hard to fill the gap. Held down two jobs; worked in a shop from nine to three, then did piecework – sewing gloves at home – at night and at weekends. She was always *there*: before I went to school; to greet me when I came home. Earned enough, so I could go to grammar school. *(shrugs sadly)* I never realized just how much she gave up. Too tied up in pursuing *my* interests.

CLAIRE. Did she have any…social life?

DONALD. In her way, visiting with her family.

CLAIRE. No male friends? Like a boyfriend?

DONALD. I don't remember any.

DAPHNE. In the nineteen-forties and fifties, people weren't as tolerant as they are now, Claire. An unwed mother was…well, looked down upon.

DONALD. Particularly true of someone who had associated with visiting troops.

CLAIRE. *(to* **DAPHNE***)* Would you have looked down on her, if you'd known her then?

DONALD. Not a fair question!

DAPHNE. *(holds up hand to* **DONALD***)* No; fair enough. *(to* **CLAIRE***)* At the time I might have. But now…no. *(slight pause)* I came to like your grandmother very much. Admired her tenacity.

DONALD. There was no social security then, like we know it now. Just welfare.

DAPHNE. *(to* **CLAIRE***)* Your grandmother would never have allowed herself to go on welfare. A very independent, resourceful woman.

DONALD. Amen! You two were good friends.

DAPHNE. She didn't interfere, and I respected that. Though I suspect there were times she didn't entirely approve of my parental abilities.

(They laugh.)

CLAIRE. I think Gran would've approved: Dad going in search of his father.

DAPHNE. I'd like to think that, too; but I have…well, reservations.

DONALD. Such as?

DAPHNE. Well…will your father – presuming there is one – will he *want* to meet you?

DONALD. I just don't know. It's the other side of the equation.

CLAIRE. It could be tricky, suddenly springing an adult son on him. A son who's already a grandfather!

DAPHNE. If...suppose...one day, next week...*(to* **DONALD***)* while you're at work, at the bank. The doorbell rings and when I open the door there's a young woman – age about 32 – standing on the doorstep...

CLAIRE. *(interrupts)* And she announces: 'Excuse me, Mrs Barlow. I'd like to speak to my father.'

(They laugh, then quickly subside into a thoughtful silence.)

(to **DAPHNE***)* How would you feel?

DAPHNE. I'd slam the frigging door in her bleeding face!

CLAIRE. *(surprised at her mother's language; her vehemence)* Mother!

DAPHNE. Cheeky bitch!

*(***DON*** thoughtfully watches their reactions.)*

CLAIRE. *(after a moment)* I'd bet you'd re-open it!

DAPHNE. No way! Why would I?

CLAIRE. Because that's how you are. You'd start wondering...

DAPHNE. I know your father better than that!

CLAIRE. Just the same....

DONALD. *(raises hand in protest)* Whatever connection is made, it won't be as blatant as that.

DAPHNE. Blatant or wrapped in cotton wool, Mrs Devereaux isn't going to take kindly to someone standing on her doorstep who's the product of her husband's pre-marital indiscretion.

CLAIRE. *(very angry)* Mother! Father was *not* the result of an indiscretion.

DAPHNE. I was trying to illustrate...

CLAIRE. *(interrupts)* Your choice of words was totally inappropriate!

DAPHNE. I was only...

CLAIRE. *(interrupts)* Gran loved him! I think he probably felt the same. The postcard.

DAPHNE. But he didn't come back. Did he?

DONALD. If he had, we wouldn't be having this discussion right now.

DAPHNE. *(goes up to* **DONALD***, places a hand on his arm)* I just want you to see what his wife would see, what she would perceive. You have to think what it might do to their relationship, their marriage.

CLAIRE. I still think your metaphor was inexcusable; unforgivable.

DONALD. Your mother makes a good point, Claire.

CLAIRE. Can you identify if he exists, without committing yourself; without forewarning him?

DONALD. There's an organization set up just to do that.

DAPHNE. Without in any way alerting him you're on the prowl?

CLAIRE. Mother! Again!

(Phone rings.)

DONALD. I won't give any names until I have that assurance. *(into phone)* Barlow here.

DAPHNE. Donald! You're not in the office!

DONALD. Oh, hello, Gordie. You all right?...No. Your mum's here...Oh....

*(**CLAIRE** reaches for phone)*

DONALD. *(cont.)* *(whispers to* **CLAIRE***)* He wants to talk to me. *(into phone)* Uh-huh...Mmmm...I'll have to go and look. Can you hang on?...No?...Then call me back in ten minutes. All right?...'Bye. *(lays phone down)* He's playing a game – something like Trivial Pursuit – wants to know which football team won the F.A. Cup in 1978. *(exits)*

CLAIRE. *(laughs lightly)* Gordie always finds some innocuous reason for phoning me, before he goes to bed.

DAPHNE. Even when he's here. I've noticed. *(slight pause)* I wish you'd brought him with you.

CLAIRE. Next week. I promise. *(slight pause)* Why are you so against Dad wanting to find his father?

DAPHNE. Why are you so 'for' it?

CLAIRE. I asked first.

DAPHNE. I don't want him to be hurt. How's he going to feel if this Devereaux man refuses to see him? To speak to him? To even acknowledge he exists? Your Dad's not as tough as he likes us to think he is.

(**CLAIRE** *nods as lights extinguish.*)

(Lights come up on Barlow living room, day, a week later. **DONALD** *and* **HOOGSTRA** *are seated.* **DONALD** *holds a brochure.)*

HOOGSTRA. *(responding to a question)* No. Connexion Closure originated in The Netherlands five years ago, by a group of people who wanted to find their fathers.

DONALD. You were one of them?

HOOGSTRA. No. My mother was.

DONALD. But now you run it? As a business?

HOOGSTRA. Three of us do.

DONALD. Did your mother find her father?

HOOGSTRA. Yes. But…he refused to see her.

DONALD. She must've been disappointed.

HOOGSTRA. Very. I'm afraid too many fathers react that way.

DONALD. Are you implying I don't have much hope?

HOOGSTRA. Not necessarily. Every case is different.

DONALD. What…um…numbers are we talking about?

HOOGSTRA. You mean the cost?

DONALD. No. That'll come later. How many are looking for their fathers?

HOOGSTRA. In the U.K. there are 25,000 people like you. Another 10,000 in the Netherlands.

DONALD. They're all looking?

HOOGSTRA. Oh, no. But the number is growing.

(Enter **DAPHNE.** **HOOGSTRA** *stands.)*

DONALD. Oh, my dear. This is Mr. Hoogstra. From Connexion Closure.

DAPHNE. How do you do, Mr. Hoogstra.

(They shake hands then sit.)

HOOGSTRA. My pleasure, Mrs. Barlow.

DONALD. *(holds up brochure)* Mr. Hoogstra has been describing…

DAPHNE. *(interrupts)* I know why he is here, Don.

HOOGSTRA. I have been explaining to Mr Barlow that many people who were fathered by Canadian serviceman now want to find out who their fathers are.

DAPHNE. Their *father is*, surely? They each have only one.

HOOGSTRA. *(disconcerted, taken aback)* Granted. Their father is.

(slight pause)

DAPHNE. Let me get this straight: you get what information you can from us, and then you send it to someone in Canada to find the father. Right?

HOOGSTRA. No, not quite. I don't send the information; I take it myself.

DAPHNE. So *you* hunt for the father?

HOOGSTRA. That is correct.

DAPHNE. And when you find him – *if* you find him – you knock on his door?

HOOGSTRA. Well, a little more gently than...

DAPHNE. Or does Mr. Barlow do that?

HOOGSTRA. No. *We* make the connections. *(to* **DONALD***)* When you give me the authority to proceed, I collect the appropriate data from you, do the research. Then, if I find him, I ask if I am to proceed further. If you say yes, I make the initial contact. That ensures absolute confidentiality: for you; and for the person you are seeking.

*(***DAPHNE*** nods approval.)*

DONALD. You mean, when you find my father, you won't tell me who he is? Or where he is?

HOOGSTRA. Quite correct. And you can rest assured that he will learn nothing about you.

DAPHNE. Except, surely, that Donald – Mr. Barlow – does exist?

HOOGSTRA. Yes. That is inevitable.

DAPHNE. And has made an enquiry?

HOOGSTRA. Correct again.

(**DAPHNE** *nods; approves.*)

DONALD. How long does it take? From the time I say 'go ahead' until you have definitive information to give me...us?

HOOGSTRA. Between two and six months.

DONALD. (*offers his mother's letter to* **HOOGSTRA**) Based on this information, how long would you say?

HOOGSTRA. (*raises hands*) No, no! I must see nothing until you are quite certain you want to do this.

DONALD. Not till I...we...decide to authorize you?

HOOGSTRA. Quite right.

DAPHNE. That, we need time to discuss.

HOOGSTRA. I understand.

DAPHNE. (*stands*) Then, as we are probably paying for your time right now...(*trails off*)

HOOGSTRA. (*laughs, stands*) No, no. There is no charge for you to make an enquiry.

DAPHNE. Quite.

DONALD. (*ushering* **HOOGSTRA** *to the door*) Shall we say I will call you within a week?

(**DONALD** *and* **HOOGSTRA** *exit.*)

HOOGSTRA. (*voice over*) That is fine. And, please, feel free to call me if you have more questions.

DONALD. (*voice over*) What if you are in Canada?

HOOGSTRA. (*voice over*) My calls are forwarded to my mobile phone, wherever I am.

(**DAPHNE** *picks up brochure, leafs through it, shakes head: she does not approve. Lights extinguish.*)

*(During the following sequence the newscaster's voice is heard over a dark stage. When lights come up, **DONALD** is sitting in an armchair, a newspaper on his lap, listening to a radio broadcast. It is nine weeks later.)*

NEWSCASTER. *(voice over)* More and more adults in their mid-fifties, who have never known their fathers, are trying to connect with them while there is still time – while their fathers are still alive. These are the sons and daughters of soldiers, sailors and airmen from overseas, who served in Britain during the war and had a liaison with a local lass. Many returned home without knowing they had fathered a child. Or, sometimes, acknowledging they had.

FEMALE INTERVIEWEE. *(voice over)* I was ecstatic when, after several months, the agency told me they had found my father. But it didn't last. A week later I was devastated to hear that he would not see me *(a catch in her voice)*; he wouldn't even admit I existed. It's like a great hole in my life and I can't do anything to fill it.

NEWSCASTER. *(voice over)* Jane's story is typical of many who are trying to find their fathers. But there is the occasional success.

MALE INTERVIEWEE. *(country accent, voice over)* I'm eating my tea when there's this phone call: A voice I'd never heard before told me he was my...

*(The phone rings. **DONALD** gets up.)*

...father, that he was in a hotel at Heathrow for the night, and could I drive there. Could I? It was only 35 miles and...

*(**DONALD** switches off radio, picks up phone.)*

DONALD. Five two eight seven one two...Oh, Mr. Hoogstra!...You found him?!...In only nine weeks?...So he does exist?...Marvelous...Where did you find him?... Oh, of course, you can't tell me...Yes. Quite right. I remember...But he does live in Canada?...Oh, you can't....Are you to go ahead? Of course you are.....

*(**DAPHNE** enters carrying a tea tray and cups.)*

No. Hold that. I need to discuss it with Mrs. Barlow... She's right here...Can you hang on?...*(pause; covers phone; to* **DAPHNE***)* Hoogstra. He's found my father!

DAPHNE. I thought as much.

DONALD. He's alive, Daph! He really does exist!

DAPHNE. *(pause while she places cups on side table, then places an arm on his sleeve)* You really want to go through with this?

DONALD. Yes. Yes, I do.

DAPHNE. You're sure?

DONALD. Just knowing he didn't die; that he's really there... That I *do* have a flesh and blood father.

DAPHNE. Isn't that enough?

DONALD. If I could just meet him, even if it's only once. It would be like filling an empty space; a vacuum. *(slight pause).* Like I'd be doing it for my mother.

DAPHNE. This is for your mother?

DONALD. *(shrugs)* In her memory, I suppose.

DAPHNE. I thought this was for *you.*

DONALD. For both of us, perhaps.

DAPHNE. Oh, Don: I'm so afraid you'll be hurt. Suppose he says "No"? Won't admit to even knowing Wendy? How will you feel about that?

DONALD. Frustrated. *(thinks a moment)* Empty.

DAPHNE. Look: the identification rate is probably pretty good. But, I fear...I'm afraid...the acceptance rate is... *(shrugs)*

DONALD. Pretty low? *(into phone)* Mr. Hoogstra? Are you there?...Right! I have a question: What would you say, on average, the acceptance rate is?...I mean, after you make contact, how many fathers agree to meet their sons?

DAPHNE. Or daughters!

DONALD. *(listens; his shoulders sag)* Less than ten percent?... Nearer five?...Hang on a minute. *(to* **DAPHNE***)* Did you...?

DAPHNE. Yes, of course. What if he says 'no'? Will you be able to live with that?

DONALD. I'd have to.

DAPHNE. No-o-o! How will you *feel*?

DONALD. Rotten.

DAPHNE. Rejected?

DONALD. *(nods)* But if I stop now, I'll live the rest of my life wondering if I should have taken the risk.

DAPHNE. Feel for ever empty?

DONALD. In a sense, yes. But, Daph, I'll always have you.

DAPHNE. You will that.

DONALD. So, what do I tell him?

DAPHNE. Oh, no! *You* have to decide.

(DONALD sighs, looks at phone; slight pause.)

If it was me, I'd probably be chicken and say 'no.' But whichever you decide, you'll have my support. You won't hear me say, 'I told you so.'

(He puts an arm around her.)

DONALD. *(into phone)* Mr. Hoogstra?…You're to go ahead. You can tell my father I want to meet him.

(Lights extinguish swiftly; perhaps a hint of Canadian music.)

*(Lights come up on Devereaux living room in North Van-
couver, January 2001. Daylight, sun shining through
French windows.* **GORDON** *stands before them, looking
at scene. Door from front hall opens; he turns and faces*
HELEN *as she ushers* **HOOGSTRA** *in and then exits [she
hears the start of the conversation].)*

HOOGSTRA. *(to* **HELEN***)* Thank you, Mrs. Devereaux. *(to*
GORDON*)* Mr. Devereaux?

GORDON. Yes…?

HOOGSTRA. My name is Paul Hoogstra. I wrote to you.

GORDON. Yes.

HOOGSTRA. I'm a researcher with Connexion Closure.

GORDON. Connection what?

HOOGSTRA. Closure. We…er…we try to make connections
between people like yourself, who had a significant
role in World War Two, and…

GORDON. *(interrupts)* I have no interest whatever in talking
to anyone about World War Two. When I returned to
Canada after the war I 'closed the book' on that part
of my life. Most of us who were closely involved in it
did.

HOOGSTRA. Of course. But, you see, sometimes there are…
er…people who want to – as you so aptly put it – to re-
open the book.

GORDON. *(peremptorily)* I am not interested.

HOOGSTRA. That is exactly the point. When someone
comes to us and says: 'I'd like you find so-and-so for
me,' then we are obliged to follow through.

GORDON. *(with emphasis)* I said no!

HOOGSTRA. That's fine. That's exactly what I need to hear.
Then when I go back to the…person…I can say you
do not wish to be contacted.

GORDON. Who is this 'person'? Who, you say, wants to…
to…?

HOOGSTRA. Contact you?

GORDON. Who *is* it?

HOOGSTRA. I regret that, at this point, I am not permitted to say.

GORDON. Is it someone I knew during the war? *(pause; no response from* HOOGSTRA*)* Someone I flew with?

HOOGSTRA. I have to respect their privacy....

GORDON. *Their* privacy! What about *my* privacy? You come waltzing in here. They clearly know about me – or you wouldn't be here – but I'm not allowed to know about them! *(reaches for phone; dials three digits)* Sounds like some form of extortion scheme...

HOOGSTRA. *(quickly holds up his hand)* No, no. It's perfectly legal, Mr. Devereaux. You are welcome to call the police, but you will find they have no reason for taking action. They are aware.

GORDON. Aware? Of what? Please explain! *(replaces phone)*

HOOGSTRA. I represent a client who just wants to know you exist. I will go back to him with no....

GORDON. Ah-ha! Him! Then it is a man!?

HOOGSTRA. *(nonplussed; he slipped)* I...I will say nothing, other than that I have found you. I will not say where you are or provide any details about you. Everything will be kept absolutely confidential.

GORDON. Yes, but what's to stop this...person – who, I presume, is paying for you to be here – what's to prevent him from following up on his own?

HOOGSTRA. We never release any information to the enquirer. We simply say we have a contact, but...

GORDON. *(interrupts)* I feel *most* uncomfortable about this. You seem to have been going behind my back, documenting information about me that is private.

HOOGSTRA. No, no. Nothing we research is confidential. Your military records are now public domain in Ottawa and are...

GORDON. Public domain?!

HOOGSTRA. ...accessible to anyone...

GORDON. Mr. Hoogstra! This interview is over! *(strides to door and opens it; signals that* HOOGSTRA *should leave)* I bid you good-day.

HOOGSTRA. I apologize for taking up your time. It is even possible that I may have found the wrong person.

GORDON. Extremely likely!

HOOGSTRA. In which case, could you either confirm or deny that...

GORDON. *(interrupts)* Of course I couldn't!

HOOGSTRA. ...that you flew with five-three-two squadron.

(**GORDON** *is clearly taken aback.*)

And in November 1944 you were on loan to the Royal Air Force for a special operation...

GORDON. *(interrupts)* How the devil did you know that?!

HOOGSTRA. It's in the R.A.F. history – at the Public Records Office – in Kew Gardens in London.

GORDON. *(closes door)* You mean to say... *(shrugs)*

HOOGSTRA. Sufficient time has passed that the records are open to anyone who knows what to ask for.

(**GORDON** *sits, nonplussed.*)

The records provide only names and dates. No technical details. Those are still secret, I expect. *(pause)* I'm sorry. I did not intend to...

GORDON. *(abruptly)* What was my military number?

HOOGSTRA. *(looks briefly at document in his hand)* It was R-two-five-three-three-zero-six when you enlisted, and J-four-eight-eight-four seven when you were commissioned.

GORDON. And my rank?

HOOGSTRA. When you flew that operation, you were a flight lieutenant *(pronounced "leff-tenant")*. You retired one year later as a squadron leader.

GORDON. And who is this person? The enquirer?...You won't tell me?

HOOGSTRA. No. I'm sorry.

GORDON. Was it Eddie Solomon? One of the pilots.

HOOGSTRA. I'm not...I can't...

GORDON. John Webster, then? My navigator *(**HOOGSTRA** shakes his head.)* Then who the hell...?

HOOGSTRA. Again, I'm sorry.

GORDON. Why would they ever want to contact me now? *(shakes head)* Unless they want to hold some sort of reunion...Ugh! Not for this guy. No. Too upsetting. See all those young men now with grey hairs. *(grim laugh)* Or lack of hair! I mean...it's all of 55 years!

HOOGSTRA. Yes. Of course. *(going carefully)* I think I can say that it isn't a military person who is enquiring...

GORDON. No?

HOOGSTRA. No.

GORDON. *(slight irony)* And of course you can't tell me his name.

HOOGSTRA. No. *(slight pause)* But I do need to identify whether you're the right person; the person he thinks you are.

GORDON. Oh, good lord!

HOOGSTRA. *(very carefully)* Would you...? Would you mind answering one or two questions?

GORDON. No. Certainly not.

HOOGSTRA. All you need to say is 'yes' or 'no.'

GORDON. I don't have to supply information?

HOOGSTRA. No. No details.

GORDON. Hmph! Then make it quick.

HOOGSTRA. In late 1944 and for the first quarter of 1945, were you stationed near Lincoln, in England?

GORDON. *(guarded)* Y-e-s.

HOOGSTRA. While you were there, did you get to meet some of the local people? I mean, people living in Lincoln.

GORDON. Well, yes. I suppose so. In the pubs mostly. We all did.

HOOGSTRA. Uh-huh. I understand the English were particularly hospitable to soldiers – er, flyers – from the Dominions.

GORDON. The *Dominions*?!

HOOGSTRA. Uh...Commonwealth.

GORDON. I should think so.

HOOGSTRA. Sorry. *(slight pause)* Er…were you ever invited into their homes?

GORDON. *(suspicious now)* Well, I suppose. Possibly. Once or twice.

HOOGSTRA. The home of Harold and Mary Barlow?

GORDON. *(defensive; the memory is there)* Is all this really necessary?

HOOGSTRA. Just one or two more…

GORDON. No…No.

HOOGSTRA. Please.

*(**GORDON** grunts.)*

Does the name Barlow come readily to mind?

GORDON. No-o-o. *(guarded now)* No…Should it?

HOOGSTRA. Possibly.

GORDON. I don't know. Really. After all these years…

HOOGSTRA. The Barlow family got to know you quite well. They'd…

GORDON. *(stands)* Mr. Hoogstra! This is getting much too personal…

HOOGSTRA. They'd invite you round for tea…

GORDON. Enough is enough!

HOOGSTRA. *(pressing on because he won't have another opportunity)* Do you remember their daughter?

GORDON. How could I possibly…?

HOOGSTRA. Wendy. Wendy Barlow. She would've been eighteen. *(holds up a snapshot-size black and white photo facing toward **GORDON**)*

GORDON. *(visibly shaken)* Enough! I said enough!

HOOGSTRA. *(quietly)* Did you know her?

GORDON. You have no right to come in here…

HOOGSTRA. *(holds up hand)* Please, Mr. Devereaux. She is not alive now. *(gently)* She died fifteen months ago.

GORDON. *(sits)* Oh. Oh. *(He is sincerely affected.)* Then I'm sorry. Did you…meet her?

HOOGSTRA. No. I wish I had.

GORDON. Did she…uh…did she leave instructions..? To contact me?

HOOGSTRA. Oh, no. Nothing like that.

GORDON. *(relieved)* Ah. *(slight pause)* Then I don't quite get the point for this…interview.

HOOGSTRA. It was her son.

GORDON. Her *son?*

HOOGSTRA. He asked me to contact you.

GORDON. But why?

HOOGSTRA. He wants to meet you.

GORDON. Why on earth would he want…? *(shakes head)*

HOOGSTRA. *(very gently)* He…he says you are his father.

GORDON. No! *(strides about)* That's impossible. Quite impossible. You go back to that young whippersnapper and tell him…*(shrugs in anger)*

HOOGSTRA. *(after a pause)* He has information that identifies you.

GORDON. *(shouts)* No!…No! No! No! Out of the question!

HOOGSTRA. I know this must come as quite a shock…

GORDON. I am *not* his father.

HOOGSTRA. Even though he has…

GORDON. *(interrupts)* I couldn't possibly be.

HOOGSTRA. He says he has proof….

GORDON. Ah, ha! He's after money. So that's it!

HOOGSTRA. No. He has no need.

GORDON. He's trumped up a scheme…

HOOGSTRA. *(breaks in)* He just wants closure.

GORDON. What do you mean: closure?

HOOGSTRA. Many adults in Britain who were fathered by Canadian servicemen, but have never known their fathers, would like to meet them. While there is still time.

GORDON. No. *(shakes head)* No. I never…I couldn't have… *(his voice rising)* And even if I was – which I insist I am not – I would not, not, not, ever want to meet him. Is that clear?

(Door enters; **HELEN** *enters tentatively from kitchen area.)*

HOOGSTRA. Quite clear.

HELEN. My dear? Is everything all right? I thought I heard someone shouting.

GORDON. *(angry)* Mr. Hoogstra, here, is just leaving.

HELEN. Oh, I'm sorry if I interrupted...*(turns back toward door, is about to leave)*

GORDON. No, Helen. Please stay. *(hardly civil, to* **HOOGSTRA***)* You were about to leave.

HOOGSTRA. Yes. *(gathers his papers, puts them in his case)* I'll just leave my card. In case you change your mind.

GORDON. Quite unnecessary.

*(***HOOGSTRA*** lays card on side table, puts his hand forward to shake, but* **GORDON** *ignores it and turns his back.* **HOOGSTRA** *turns to* **HELEN***.)*

HOOGSTRA. Well, goodbye Mrs. Devereaux.

HELEN. Yes. Goodbye.

*(***HELEN*** and* **HOOGSTRA** *exit.* **GORDON** *stands, pensive.* **HELEN** *re-enters, walks to table, picks up card.)*

My dear. What was that all about?

GORDON. Just someone who should know better.

HELEN. *(reading card)* Connexion Closure. What a strange way to spell connexion: with an 'x.'

GORDON. That just about says it all.

(She waits for him to continue, but he doesn't.)

HELEN. Whatever did he want, Gordon? To make you so angry? *(she goes up to him, places a hand on his arm)* You're still angry. You're trembling.

GORDON. Oh, he...er...he wanted me to set up a meeting, a sort of re-connection...

HELEN. With the men you used to fly with?

GORDON. *(nods)* You know how I feel about that!

HELEN. *(smiles)* You 'closed the door.' Back in 1945.

*(**GORDON** nods.)*

(waggles card) Ah, now I see the connection. But not the 'x.'

GORDON. In England, it can be an alternative spelling.

HELEN. Really?

GORDON. Some of the newspapers use it.

HELEN. But…why should this…*(looks at card)* Mr. Hoogstra, make you so angry?

GORDON. He was so insistent. Wouldn't take no for an answer.

HELEN. Hmmm…Time for that before-dinner dry martini. Don't you think?

GORDON. Bit early, isn't it?

HELEN. Oh, I don't think so.

*(Without **GORDON** noticing her do it, she tucks **HOOG-STRA**'s card up her sleeve or into a pocket, then exits. **GORDON** sits, stares pensively in front of him, shaken by what has just occurred.)*

(Lights extinguish slowly.)

(Lights come up on the Barlow living room three weeks later; night. **DONALD** *and* **HOOGSTRA** *are seated.)*

HOOGSTRA. I wanted to see you personally, not just write a letter.

DONALD. I appreciate that.

HOOGSTRA. Sometimes it can be so difficult. *(sighs)* Each time I embark on a search – as I have for you – I try to maintain my distance; remain objective. But, when I visited your father, it was almost impossible not to feel guilty; that it should be you, not me, walking in through his door.

DONALD. You did get to talk to him?

HOOGSTRA. Oh, yes.

DONALD. Was he...I don't know quite how to say it...Was he as difficult as you led me to believe?

HOOGSTRA. *(slight hesitation)* He was...adamant...*(slight pause)*

DONALD. That he didn't want to see me?

HOOGSTRA. Yes.

DONALD. Was he shocked? To discover that I exist...?

HOOGSTRA. He didn't believe me. Most don't. They say it must have been someone else.

DONALD. No...Not in my case. You've seen my mother's letter.

HOOGSTRA. Yes.

DONALD. So he shut the door in your face? My face.

HOOGSTRA. Definitely. Physically and emotionally.

DONALD. Did you meet anyone else?

HOOGSTRA. You mean, related to him?

DONALD. Yes.

HOOGSTRA. I cannot tell you anything more than I have. I'm sorry.

DONALD. Understood. *(slight pause)* I appreciated your phone call. The day after you saw him.

HOOGSTRA. I felt you should know right away, rather than go on hoping, waiting. *(shrugs)*

(Car lights sweep past window.)

DONALD. Ah! That will be my wife. And our grandson.

HOOGSTRA. Then I must prepare to leave. Is there anything else you need to know?

DONALD. Do you think – did you sense – he might possibly change his mind?

HOOGSTRA. Frankly, no.

DONALD. But you left the door open, just a crack?

HOOGSTRA. Of course. He knows how to get hold of me.

DONALD. Thank you.

HOOGSTRA. You are not alone. Almost everyone we interview…

(Door opens. Enter **GORDIE,** *who runs to* **DONALD** *and gives him a hug.)*

GORDIE. Grandpa!

DONALD. How are you, Gordie?

GORDIE. Brilliant! Can I stay the night?…Please?

DONALD. Whoa! This is Mr Hoogstra. He is from the Netherlands. *(to* **HOOGSTRA***)* My grandson, Gordie.

GORDIE. *(extends hand; speaks slowly and distinctly, in Dutch:)* Hoe gaab het ermee? *("How do you do?")*

HOOGSTRA. *(slightly taken aback; in Dutch)* Heel goed; en u? *("Very well. And you?")*

GORDIE. *(in Dutch)* Goed, dank u. *("Good, thank you")* *(laughs; in English)* Brilliant.

DONALD. Where did you learn…?

GORDIE. At school. There are two Dutch boys in my class. Twins.

HOOGSTRA. You speak well.

GORDIE. Thanks. But that's all I know, really. Except for some swear words.

(laughter)

HOOGSTRA. Then, I think this is an appropriate moment for me to depart.

DONALD. Thank you for taking the time.

*(***DONALD** *and* **HOOGSTRA** *exit.* **GORDIE** *picks up a book, climbs onto sofa, turns pages, whistles. His actions show he is comfortable in his grandparents' home.)*

(Enter **DONALD** *and* **CLAIRE.** *)*

DONALD. No, Claire. He's a good man. He did what he could. He could have just sent me a letter.

*(***CLAIRE** *mimes 'Keep Quiet' and points to* **GORDIE.** *)*

(sotto voice) He doesn't know?

CLAIRE. *(quietly)* It's better he doesn't.

DONALD. *(nods; slight pause)* Gordie asked if he could sleep over.

GORDIE. I don't have any school tomorrow. Mum? Please?

CLAIRE. Is it all right with you and Mum?

DONALD. I think so. We have nothing particular planned.

CLAIRE. It would help. I have an interview in Manchester.

(Enter **DAPHNE.** *)*

DAPHNE. Right. *(to* **GORDIE***)* I've switched on the electric blanket in your bed.

DONALD. You mean, you already discussed…

GORDIE. *(jumps in)* In the car. Gran said I was to ask you.

DONALD. Fine. Fine. Then you can make my breakfast in the morning.

GORDIE. Cool! Poached eggs?

DONALD. You know the routine.

DAPHNE. *(to* **GORDIE***)* Are you hungry?

GORDIE. A bit.

CLAIRE. Of course!

DAPHNE. Come on. We'll raid the refrigerator. See what appeals to you.

GORDIE. *(as he and* **DAPHNE** *exit)* Do you have any Haagen-Daz?

DAPHNE. *(voice over, as door closes)* Oh, I expect.

DONALD. You haven't told Gordie?

CLAIRE. Nothing.

DONALD. You don't think he should know?

CLAIRE. No. Let him remember his great-grandmother as he knew her. Let's not spoil the image by implying she had a…I was going to say 'wayward moment'…a previous love. Mum agrees.

DONALD. All right. I'll be careful.

(**CLAIRE** *sits, unsure how to address an idea she needs to present to* **DONALD**.)

CLAIRE. Dad: I'm sorry. I'm really sorry. You must have felt so…disappointed.

DONALD. Frustrated, mostly. And angry…that he should be so selfish; so short-sighted.

CLAIRE. That he let the moment…the possibility…just drop?

DONALD. Oh, Claire, it was a nice idea, but it just didn't work out. I think I knew all along what the result would be.

CLAIRE. But you still kept hoping?

DONALD. I suppose.

CLAIRE. I could tell, when you phoned, the hurt in your voice.

DONALD. It's over now. I've come to terms with it. So let's sign off the chapter on that little episode, shall we? Talk no more about it.

(*slight pause*)

CLAIRE. I don't think you need to 'sign off the chapter' yet.

DONALD. Don't, Claire.

CLAIRE. I would like to…

DONALD. Please, Claire!

CLAIRE. …take it just one step further.

DONALD. Claire! Drop it!

CLAIRE. (*rises; paces; nervous energy*) Can you give me ten minutes?

DONALD. Not if it's about contacting my father.

CLAIRE. It isn't. Not directly.

DONALD. Then, no.

CLAIRE. It's only a segment of a much larger project.

(**DONALD** *raises his hand 'no' and shakes his head.*)

And the segment can be omitted if you're not comfortable with it. Though, I admit, it promises to be the most exciting episode of the series.

(**DONALD** *looks at her suspiciously.*)

Hear me out.

DONALD. Well, sit down then, for Pete's sake!

CLAIRE. *(sits, leans forward)* In about six months' time we're going to start publishing a series called 'Where Are They Now?' About people who made the news once, but now have faded into the background. *(changes pace)* By the way, this is hush-hush, while we're doing the research. We don't want a competing publication to get wind of the idea and jump the gun on us.

DONALD. I understand. But I don't see how...*(shrugs)*

CLAIRE. Bear with me, Dad. One of the projects is about the original heart transplant patients, and the doctors who performed the operations. *(dramatically)* Where Are They Now? How many survived? Of those who did, how has it affected their lives?

DONALD. I know of only one.

CLAIRE. Right! But there are others. Another's hunting down triplets, now in their forties and fifties. Do a story on what their lives have been like, and whether their dependence on each other continued into middle age. *(slight pause)* My editor's asking for proposals on other topics, and I've got a great one.

DONALD. You're not suggesting...?

CLAIRE. Your story? No. What I want to write about occurred before my time; yours, too. Do you remember hearing about a special rescue mission that took place in Belgium late in 1944?

(**DONALD** *shakes his head 'no.' From her briefcase she pulls out a folder with maps and photographs, sits beside him, and refers to specific pages as she speaks.*)

As the Allied armies advanced into Europe, pushing the Nazi army back towards Germany, there was a fear they might execute some high-level nuclear physicists being held in a castle – a prison, really – somewhere near Bruges. So the Allies set up a special two-level task force: the air force would breach a hole in the castle walls and disable the guards by bombing their quarters

– to be done at night, while they slept – but without harming the prisoners. At the same time a commando unit would be parachuted in nearby, to go in through the hole and bring the prisoners out.

We want to research what happened to those prisoners: people like Rene Tetreault, Johan Hagenborg. But that's only half the story. We also want to find the flyers – a very select group – who mounted the attack. At the time it was a big item in the news, because it was dangerous and required precise marksmanship. But… Where Are They Now?

DONALD. How are you going to get your information?

CLAIRE. At the Public Records Office at Kew.

DONALD. *Military* records?

CLAIRE. Under the 'right to know' act, they're released after thirty years. Except the very, very secret ones, like the bomb used for the Mohne and Eder dams.

DONALD. How do you know all this?

CLAIRE. I've been there, started my research. I'm doing the flyers. Margery Atkinson's researching the prisoners.

DONALD. But how are you going to find them after…more than fifty years?!

CLAIRE. That's what a researcher does. I've already found one of them. In Manchester. But I've got to move fast, they're already into their mid-to-late-seventies.

DONALD. Humph. Good luck!

CLAIRE. I'll not find all of them, I know. But I will find the ones who are still alive. *(slight pause)* There is one other thing. One of those pilots is Gordon Devereaux.

DONALD. My father? Oh, no. Oh, no. You're not doing that!

CLAIRE. I can't avoid it, Dad!

DONALD. Have you been talking to Paul Hoogstra?

CLAIRE. No…

DONALD. Behind my back?

CLAIRE. No. No way. I want to do this on my own.

DONALD. Not without my say-so!

CLAIRE. *(looks quizzically at him)* The story will be incomplete.

DONALD. Then it will just have to be.

CLAIRE. He was the flight leader – first on the target. He led the other planes in.

DONALD. I don't like this one bit. Anyway, as soon as he hears your voice – your English accent – he'll smell a rat. He's bound to.

CLAIRE. Of course he will! But I'll wager he won't say anything. He'll just be cautious at first, until he sees I really am a writer on a project.

(**DONALD** *shakes head; doubtful.*)

Why would he make a connection? I'll be using my married name. I have to. Even after the divorce I won't be able to change it. It's my byline in the mag: Claire Summers, staff writer….

DONALD. Claire! Stop! Are you trying to accomplish what Hoogstra couldn't? Trying to prove something?

CLAIRE. No. I have a good story and…

DONALD. *(demanding)* Which came first: my contact with Hoogstra or your idea for this story?

CLAIRE. Hoogstra. I have to admit that.

DONALD. And is that what prompted you to research this story?

CLAIRE. No. I was just trying to find a meaningful incident. From the war. Something that hit the news, captured readers' imagination. I hunted through newspapers, from 1941 onward…

DONALD. *(interrupts)* Why not the Dam Busters – six one seven squadron – their raid on the dams you mentioned? Famous.

CLAIRE. Too famous. Numerous films and stories already. Even you know the number of the squadron.

DONALD. Pity. Then we wouldn't be having this argument!

CLAIRE. Argument? No. Difference of opinion, perhaps.

DONALD. *(smiles: the first time he has relaxed; slight pause)* What about the raid on Dieppe? That was a Canadian story, if ever there was.

CLAIRE. Too Canadian. If we had a Canadian circulation, then I'd've said yes. But we don't. *(slight pause)* It wasn't until I came across reports of the Bruges raid; the sheer audacity of it...

DONALD. *(interrupts)* And that's when you came across the name Devereaux?

CLAIRE. No. Not at first. It wasn't until I saw his name listed as one of the pilots...

DONALD. *(interrupts)* So why didn't you stop? Right then?

CLAIRE. I was in a quandary. Ethically, I felt I should just drop the idea. But was it an 'ethical' issue? As a journalist I have to be objective, keep my distance...

(Enter **DAPHNE.** *)*

...Not let my heart dictate. *(to* **DAPHNE***)* Where's Gordie?

DAPHNE. Sitting at my computer, with his new game.

CLAIRE. Another game? You spoil him.

DONALD. Why not? He's our only grandson.

DAPHNE. In my day we were bought books as a treat. Now it's software.

DONALD. Times change.

DAPHNE. *(to* **CLAIRE***)* Well? Did you?

CLAIRE. Not decided yet.

DONALD. *(to* **DAPHNE***)* You know?

DAPHNE. Claire mentioned it. In the car, while we were waiting for Gordie.

DONALD. *(a bit put out)* Humph. Have I been set up?

DAPHNE. No, no...we can only...*(overlapping)*

CLAIRE. I wasn't trying...

*(***CLAIRE*** indicates for* **DAPHNE** *to continue.)*

DAPHNE. Claire just gave me a bare-bones overview of what she had in mind.

CLAIRE. I wasn't trying to persuade Mum first.

DAPHNE. Frankly, I'm not happy about this. Most uncomfortable.

DONALD. *(to* CLAIRE*)* Is it your intention to go in and do what that Dutch man was unable to do?

CLAIRE. No. Definitely not. I just want to go in and get a story: describe who Devereaux is...what he did...and what he's done since. If possible, if he'll permit, get his impression of the raid – fifty-six years later.

DONALD. But all the time you will be looking for an opportunity to...

CLAIRE. *(interrupts)* No. No. You've never seen me at an interview, Dad. I can be...I am...totally focused. Fully professional.

DAPHNE. I can believe that.

DONALD. But you can't deny, if the opportunity arose, you'd use it to say to him: 'Oh, hi! Did you know I'm your granddaughter?'

CLAIRE. No. I don't plan to. The atmosphere would have to be extraordinarily conducive before I would even attempt to identify myself. And I certainly wouldn't say it like that!

DAPHNE. I should hope not.

DONALD. How much research have you done?

CLAIRE. About the raid: a lot. About the individual pilots and navigators: virtually none.

DONALD. When do you plan to start?

CLAIRE. Soon, for the R.A.F. pilots. In a few months, for the two Canadian crews. I don't plan to go to Canada until August.

DAPHNE. Claire wants to combine the trip with a holiday.

CLAIRE. As soon as Gordie's out of school for the summer.

DONALD. *(taken aback)* You're taking Gordie?

CLAIRE. Of course.

DONALD. When you go to interview Devereaux?

DAPHNE. Would that be wise...?

CLAIRE. *(very firm, almost strident)* Gordie knows absolutely nothing about any...'connections.' And I plan to keep it that way. As far as Gordie's concerned, it will be just one of three or four interviews I expect to conduct over there. Of no special significance.

DONALD. I think you're overlooking an important factor. How do you know these people are still living in Canada?

DAPHNE. Or *if* they're still living?

CLAIRE. True. Although I know one is: Gordon Devereaux.

DONALD. *(strides about)* I don't like it, Claire. Not at all. But...am I in a position to prevent you?

DAPHNE. *(thoughtfully, to* DONALD*)* At first, when you were making arrangements with that Mr...

DONALD. Hoogstra.

DAPHNE. Hoogstra...I was very hesitant. I was concerned you would have such high expectations that you'd be more than just 'upset' if your father, predictably, rejected you.

CLAIRE. And you were.

DONALD. I agree: I was.

DAPHNE. Now my fear is bouncing right back. I know – before – I said :'All right, try it.' But...*(to* CLAIRE*)* I don't want your father to get his hopes up...

CLAIRE. No, no...

DAPHNE. ...to have to walk that tightrope – to be on edge – all over again.

(CLAIRE *and* DAPHNE *are clearly confrontational.)*

CLAIRE. I don't intend to say anything that will...

DAPHNE. It's...just...not...fair!

(Awkward pause.)

DONALD. I'm over it now, Daph.

DAPHNE. Are you? *(shakes head)*

DONALD. I can't see much harm in Claire calling on him, *(to* CLAIRE*)* but *only* in a professional sense...

CLAIRE. That goes without saying.

(Slight pause; DAPHNE *shakes her head.)*

DONALD. Can you guarantee you'll maintain your distance? That you won't let your emotions get the better of you? Obscure why you're really there?

CLAIRE. I'll be there *only* to interview him...

DAPHNE. *(interrupts)* So easy to say!

CLAIRE. I wouldn't do it any other way!

DAPHNE. I wish you'd...

(GORDIE *enters and runs up to* DAPHNE.)

GORDIE. I scored twenty-eight thousand, six hundred and sixty-five!

DAPHNE. Brilliant!

GORDIE. And that's at level three!

DAPHNE. You mastered it fast.

DONALD. *(puts hand on* CLAIRE*'s shoulder)* Gordie: your mother was sharing an idea with us...

CLAIRE. *(cautioning him)* Dad!

DONALD. Can I tell him?

CLAIRE. Bit late to ask that now!

(slight pause)

DAPHNE. *(to* DONALD*)* You mean, you've decided it's all right for Claire to...

CLAIRE. *(interrupts)* Mum! It's *Dad's* decision...

(CLAIRE *and* DAPHNE *are again confrontational.*)

DAPHNE. Is it really? Don't you care how much you could hurt your father?

CLAIRE. I told you, I'm not...

DAPHNE. You're callous! Just interested in what you're...

DONALD. Please, you two. That's enough. *(to* CLAIRE, *inclining his head toward* GORDIE*)* Go ahead.

DAPHNE. I can't believe you'd...

DONALD. *(gently, to* DAPHNE*)* Easy, Daph.

(DAPHNE *throws her hands up in despair, moves toward door, as if to exit.* GORDIE *is upset by her outburst.*)

GORDIE. Gran...?

(DAPHNE *pauses, turns back.*)

DAPHNE. It's all right, Gordie. *(sits beside him; to* DONALD*)* You make your bed; you lie in it.

DONALD. *(sighs; to* CLAIRE, *inclines head toward* GORDIE*)* Shall I...?

*(*CLAIRE *nods.)*

(to GORDIE*)* Your mother wants to take you on holiday with her next summer; overseas...

GORDIE. *(excited, looks at* DONALD *and* CLAIRE*)* To Japan? Japan?

DONALD. Why Japan?

CLAIRE. They're studying Japan at school. *(to* GORDIE*)* I thought, maybe, you and I should take a look at Canada...

GORDIE. *(enthusiastic)* Canada!

CLAIRE. For three weeks.

GORDIE. Can we go to Niagara Falls?

CLAIRE. I expect so...

GORDIE. There's a boat goes right under the falls, in the mist. I saw it on telly.

CLAIRE. When we fly into Toronto, I guess. We could take a tour. Go on to Windsor from there.

DONALD. Windsor? Something from when I was at school: Geography!...The only city in Canada that is *south* – on the other side of a river – of an American city...

CLAIRE. Right! Detroit.

GORDIE. Detroit!! Home of the Red Wings!

DONALD. *(to* DAPHNE*)* A hockey team...

GORDIE. *(to* CLAIRE*)* Could we see them play?

DONALD. Wrong time of the year, old son, August. Hockey's for the winter.

GORDIE. A-a-ah. That's where Gordie Howe used to skate!

CLAIRE. *(slight irony, but with humour)* Oh, yes...Gordie Howe.

(CURTAIN)

ACT 2

(Lights come up on the Devereaux residence in North Vancouver; afternoon, August 2001. GORDON *sits reading newspaper, classical music on stereo;* HELEN *opens door from front hall.)*

HELEN. There's a young woman here…

GORDON. I heard the bell.

HELEN. From England, I think, by the voice.

GORDON. *(suspicious)* Humph.

HELEN. *(reads* CLAIRE*'s card)* Claire Summers. Staff Writer. Collishawe Press. Slough, Berks. *(she says: 'Sluff, Berks)*

GORDON. I think they say Slough and Berkshire. *(as in 'plow' and 'Barks')*

HELEN. *(shrugs)* Pardon me!

GORDON. She wrote. *(picks up letter from side table)*

HELEN. Am I to send her packing?

GORDON. No. I'll take a chance.

HELEN. She sounds genuine enough.

GORDON. So did that Dutchman, six months ago.

*(*HELEN *exits;* GORDON *switches off stereo;* HELEN *and* CLAIRE *enter from front hall;* GORDON *stands when* CLAIRE *enters.)*

CLAIRE. Mr. Devereaux? How do you do?

GORDON. Good to meet you, Ms. Summers. *(indicates she should sit)* Do you prefer to be called Ms. or Mrs. – or Miss?

CLAIRE. Well, actually I prefer 'Claire.' But, to answer your question: Ms. is preferable to Mrs.

HELEN. Oh, no, I *like* to be known as *Mrs.* Devereaux. It tells people who I am.

CLAIRE. Yes, of course. *(slight pause;* **CLAIRE** *looks out of French windows)* You live in a lovely city.

GORDON. Your first time in Vancouver?

CLAIRE. Yes. An eye-opener! Mountains right on your door-step!

HELEN. Do you ski?

CLAIRE. A little.

HELEN. We can be on the slopes in thirty minutes.

GORDON. In the winter.

CLAIRE. Of course.

GORDON. And no snow down here!

HELEN. *(leads her to window)* Mount Seymour. Right up there!

GORDON. When you can see it. You're lucky. There are many days when the mountains are obscured by cloud.

HELEN. You wouldn't know they were there.

GORDON. One of the penalties of living on the north shore.

HELEN. Would you like something to drink? I was about to make iced tea.

CLAIRE. That would be lovely. Thank you.

HELEN. Gordon?

GORDON. Yes. Yes. Me too.

> **(HELEN** *exits to kitchen side of house.* **GORDON** *indicates for* **CLAIRE** *to sit.)*
>
> Now, Ms. Summers…

CLAIRE. Oh, Claire, please.

GORDON. Your reason for being here. *(holds up letter)* Tell me about this…er…project you're involved with.

CLAIRE. As I said in my letter, *(She reaches into her briefcase and pulls out a copy of the magazine 'The Source')* I'm a staff writer for *The Source*. It's a middle-road publication, half way between *The Economist* and *Company Magazine*. *(sees* **GORDON** *does not recognize the second name)* A bit like your Maclean's.

GORDON. Ah!

CLAIRE. We report on historical events, semi-recent history, inverviews with people who once were involved with a major event, get their perspective on the event, as they saw it then and as they see it now.

GORDON. Can you be more precise? Give me an example?

CLAIRE. *(she hands him the magazine)* Take a look at the two-page spread on pages 8 and 9...*(pauses, while* **GORDON** *searches)*

GORDON. 'Where Are They Now?'?

CLAIRE. Right.

GORDON. By Claire Summers.

CLAIRE. My most recent effort. It traces four sets of triplets, two of them well known to readers in the U.K., two totally unknown. How life has treated them; how intensely they have stayed connected; whether they feel different to other people in their age group.

GORDON. I see. *(pause while he reads)* And your focus now is...?

CLAIRE. The R.A.F.'s daring raid on the Nazi prison in a castle near Bruges, November 1944.

GORDON. I see. *(closes magazine suddenly)* I should tell you that I never give interviews about what I did in the war – it's a matter of principle. I have never revisited the war years with anyone since I was demobilized in 1945, not even with my wife or our two daughters. When I took off my uniform for the last time, I 'shut the hangar door', so to speak.

CLAIRE. Did you keep your uniform? Do you still have it?

GORDON. What a strange question! Much too personal. If that's how you conduct your interviews, we might as well...*(close the door right now)*

CLAIRE. *(breaks in)* I'm sorry. I didn't mean to offend. It's just that Patrice LePage kept his. Flight Lieutenant Patrice LePage, I should say. He *wanted* to show...

GORDON. *(interrupts)* You've talked to Patrice?

CLAIRE. At Ancienne Lorette, in Quebec.

GORDON. Good lord! My navigator trained at Ancienne Lorette.

CLAIRE. John Webster?

GORDON. You've talked to him, too?

CLAIRE. Not yet. On my way home. I wanted to see you first.

GORDON. Why me?

CLAIRE. You were pilot in charge. You led the raid. You were the first to fly into the target.

GORDON. How on earth did you know that?

CLAIRE. Flight Lieutenant Waggoner.

GORDON. Charlie? Charlie Waggoner?

CLAIRE. He's a doctor now.

GORDON. Slap-dash Charlie? A doctor?

CLAIRE. Semi-retired. Lives in Devon. Dawlish, to be exact. I can give you his address.

GORDON. No, no! I don't want to…er…No.

CLAIRE. I understand.

GORDON. No. I don't think you do.

(Pause; he walks to window, looks out, turns back to her; **CLAIRE** *waits.)*

What we did…what we were made to do…The damage we did…the deaths we caused…what happened to my friends: the men I flew with. No. All I wanted to do was erase it from my memory, as best I could. Start again.

(pause)

CLAIRE. Which you did.

GORDON. Yes. It was difficult, but I had help. Helen – my wife – and the children. Helen knew not to probe, not to ask questions. The children just didn't know…never asked. *(pause)* Frankly, Ms. Summers, I don't think you have picked the right man.

CLAIRE. *(after a moment; very carefully)* I think I probably did. Our readers want to know what happened to people who once, very briefly, were in the news – as you were, fifty-seven years ago – and then dropped completely out of sight. Very strong human-interest stories; make compelling reading.

GORDON. I really don't think...

CLAIRE. *(interrupts)* It's not my intention to delve into – explore – painful moments. I just want to write a story that describes what happened next. Show readers there *is* a life after...

GORDON. *(interrupts)* And then I'll be besieged by people wanting to know more, banging on our door and expecting me to *want* to go back to....

(HELEN enters, bearing a tray of drinks.)

Our privacy will be destroyed.

CLAIRE. We can protect your identity; conceal your location. That would be your choice. And, you have to remember, *(picks up magazine)* 'The Source' is sold only in the U.K. Nobody will see it here.

(Slight pause as HELEN hands out drinks.)

HELEN. I never asked if you take sugar.

CLAIRE. Yes, please.

(HELEN passes bowl around.)

HELEN. Will you be staying long in Vancouver?

CLAIRE. About five days. We want to drive up to Whistler Mountain, and take the ferry over to Victoria.

HELEN. Be sure to visit Butchart Gardens while you're there. Glorious display.

CLAIRE. It's on our list.

HELEN. We? Our? Your husband is with you?

CLAIRE. Er...no. Just my son.

HELEN. And how old is he?

CLAIRE. Nine.

HELEN. And where is he now?

GORDON. *(cautionary)* Helen, it's hardly our business...

CLAIRE. Waiting in the car.

HELEN. *(appalled)* You didn't bring him in? You left him in the car?

CLAIRE. I parked in the shade. Under a tree.

HELEN. But he's only nine!

CLAIRE. He's used to it. He has his iPod and his Game Boy: one of those handheld computer games.

HELEN. Oh, you should have brought him in! Shouldn't she, Gordon?

(GORDON *raises his arms in shrugged agreement.*)

CLAIRE. I thought, as Mr. Devereaux and I had business to discuss, it would be better for us to be on our own.

HELEN. Oh, no! That's not right. He could come into the solarium with me. Now, you just go out there and bring him in.

CLAIRE. *(laughs)* Oh, all right. *(she's a little relieved, really; she exits through hall door.)*

GORDON. Helen, you shouldn't…

HELEN. Nonsense. He's only nine.

GORDON. A nine-year-old today is much more street-smart than when our two were nine.

HELEN. Just the same, he's a visitor. We should make him feel at home. *(looks at* GORDON*'s raised eyebrows)* Well, I should, anyway.

(GORDON *laughs.*)

Is she all right? *(indicates chair where* CLAIRE *was sitting)* Genuine?

GORDON. *(carefully, with growing confidence)* Yes. I think she is.

HELEN. It's just a coincidence that, six months ago…?

GORDON. Yes. It seems to be. She *is* a writer *(points to magazine)*. And she's not pushy, like he was. And she does know her stuff.

HELEN. Then you'll let her interview you?

GORDON. Probably.

HELEN. Write about you?

GORDON. Possibly.

HELEN. Here they come.

(CLAIRE *and* GORDIE *enter through hall door; she has a hand on his shoulder.*)

CLAIRE. Gordie: this is Mr. and Mrs. Devereaux.

(GORDIE *steps toward them, hand held forward.*)

GORDIE. How do you do, Mrs. Devereaux.

(*They shake hands.*)

HELEN. I'm glad to meet you...Gordie.

GORDIE. How do you do, Mr. Devereaux.

GORDON. My pleasure, Gordie.

(*slight pause*)	**GORDIE.**
Is Gordie short for...?	Did you really fly...?

(*They stop, with slight, embarrassed smiles.*)

GORDIE. I'm sorry, sir. You were already speaking.

GORDON. Well, I was just surprised...

HELEN. (*intervenes*) I think Mr Devereaux was asking if Gordie is short for 'Gordon.'

GORDIE. Oh, no. I don't think so...(*appeals to* CLAIRE) I'm just 'Gordie,' aren't I, Mum?

CLAIRE. You certainly are. (*she is caught off guard, not having realized the similarity in their names*) It was your father's choice. (*to* GORDON *and* HELEN) His father idolized Gordie Howe, the Canadian hockey player.

HELEN. Ah, yes. I'm not a hockey fan myself, but the name is familiar.

GORDON. It's Wayne Gretzki today. He's retired from hockey – retired young – but his name's still on everyone's lips.

GORDIE. My Dad's writing a...a history of Gordie Howe.

CLAIRE. (*irony*) If he ever gets around to it!

GORDIE. Right now he's on safari somewhere in South Africa.

CLAIRE. As a tour guide.

HELEN. Well, you certainly have travelled in different directions!

CLAIRE. I suppose you could put it like that.

(**HELEN** *suspects the family is coming apart, does not comment.* **GORDIE** *has been looking at the pictures on the walls.*)

GORDIE. *(to* **GORDON***; he's a little disappointed)* You don't have a picture of a Mosquito?

HELEN. We don't get many mosquitoes in Vancouver.

GORDON. I think Gordie is referring to a certain type of airplane, Helen. *(to* **GORDIE***)* Am I right?

GORDIE. The deHavilland Mosquito. Made of plywood. Two Merlin engines.

GORDON. Where did you learn that?!

GORDIE. In the library. After Mummy talked to Mr. Waggoner.

GORDON. Good lord! *(to* **CLAIRE***, suspicious)* What have you told him?

CLAIRE. Very little. *(takes* **GORDIE***'s arm)* Later, Gordie; later…

GORDIE. Did you fly the Mark 4 or Mark 16?

GORDON. The Mark 16, if I remember correctly. No. Both really, at different times.

GORDIE. Cool! Was there a twenty-millimetre cannon, sort of at knee level, between you and the navigator?

GORDON. *(amazed at his knowledge)* Sometimes. It depended on the type of operation, what kind of flying we had to do.

HELEN. *(trying to change direction of the conversation)* Oh, my, Gordie. How thoughtless of me! We all seem to have cool drinks, and I haven't offered you one. Why don't you come with me, see what we can find?

GORDIE. Oh, yes, please. Do you have coke?

HELEN. Coca Cola?

GORDIE. Is that all right, Mum?

(**CLAIRE** *nods.* **HELEN** *and* **GORDIE** *move toward kitchen door and exit.*)

(voice over) What do you call your cat?

HELEN. *(voice over)* Mimsy. We don't allow her in the living room She uses the furniture as a scratching post.

CLAIRE. I'm sorry, Mr. Devereaux. Gordie wasn't very tactful.

GORDON. He wasn't to know, I guess.

CLAIRE. I'll caution him, not to talk about your flying.

GORDON. *(a little shrug)* Perhaps. If you must. But, I was intrigued: where did he learn so much?

CLAIRE. Gordie's like a sponge. When there's something he's interested in, something he really wants to know, he homes right in on it; won't let go.

GORDON. You're sure you didn't prepare him? Prompt him, before you came?

CLAIRE. For heaven's sake, no. When I knew he'd be travelling with me, I told him about the raid: why it was necessary and what it achieved. Just the basics. I can't keep saying: 'What I'm doing is secret, so don't ask questions.' He'd want to ask all that much more.

GORDON. Well, he's got his facts, right. Took me by surprise.

CLAIRE. It started shortly after we met Mr. Waggoner. He has model aeroplanes strung up all over the house. Gordie couldn't take his eyes off them.

GORDON. I regret I don't have any: not quite my thing. And our grandchildren have no interest whatsoever. *(picks up his glass)* Suppose we sit out in the verandah for this interview. Much more pleasant.

CLAIRE. Right. *(picks up her glass)*

(**GORDON** *stands back to let her through door first. As she does so, he says:)*

GORDON. I did keep my uniform.

(**CLAIRE** *laughs.)*

(*Lights extinguish.)*

*(Lights come up on Barlow living room, in darkness —
it's just after midnight. Streetlight effect through window.
Portable phone rings. After several rings, DONALD enters
wearing a dressing gown, switches on lights, searches for
phone, picks it up.)*

DONALD. Five two eight seven one two....Oh! Hello, Claire!
Just a minute, I'll call your mother. *(He takes phone from
ear, goes to door and opens it; calls up the stairs.)* Daphne!
It's Claire. Calling from Canada.

DAPHNE. *(distant voice off)* At this time of night?

DONALD. *(into phone)* Where are you?.... Vancouver?...They
tell me it's beautiful.

(DAPHNE enters, dressing gown over nightdress.)

DAPHNE. I do think she might call at a more reasonable
time.

DONALD. *(signals for DAPHNE to pick up regular phone on side
table)* It's the time difference.

DAPHNE. Humph! *(picks up phone)* Claire?

*(Lights come up on small corner of motel bedroom: bed,
side table, telephone, lamp. CLAIRE sits on bed, phone to
her ear.)*

CLAIRE. Hello, Mum.

DAPHNE. What time is it there?

CLAIRE. Just after four p.m. Did I get the time wrong
again?

DONALD. There's an eight-hour time difference. It's eight
minutes after midnight here.

CLAIRE. I'm so sorry. You were in bed, weren't you?

DONALD. Just reading. You didn't wake us up.

DAPHNE. *(sotto voice, to DONALD)* Not you, maybe! *(into
phone)* Is this about Gordie? Is he all right, Claire?

CLAIRE. *(laughs)* He's fine, Mum. Brilliant. He's having a
ball.

DAPHNE. Is he there? Can I speak to him?

CLAIRE. No. I'm sorry. He's out.

DAPHNE. Out? How can he be 'out'? You're on your own with him, and you say he's 'out'?

CLAIRE. He's fine, Mum. He's in good hands.

DAPHNE. I don't understand how you can...

CLAIRE. *(interrupts)* I wouldn't've called if I'd known you were going to question my judgment.

(awkward pause)

DONALD. As long as he's all right.

DAPHNE. *(miffed)* Is it appropriate to ask *where* he is? And with whom?

CLAIRE. Of course. But I was going to tell you anyway. *(pause)* He's gone fishing.

DONALD. Fishing?

CLAIRE. At Horseshoe Bay. A ferry port about eighteen kilometres north of Vancouver. It's very pretty. Scenic.

DAPHNE. And who, may I ask, is he with?

CLAIRE. A special pal. *(pause; waits; almost a giggle)* His great-grandfather.

DONALD. Mr. Devereaux?

DAPHNE. What have you...?

DONALD. *(over-riding her)* You mean, he knows?

CLAIRE. No. Not at all.

DAPHNE. I don't understand how you could possibly...

CLAIRE. Mum! Listen a moment, will you! This conversation has gone all topsy-turvy. I called to let you know everything's going fine – for Gordie and for me, with the interview. We've been in Vancouver three days and we're having a brilliant time.

DONALD. Well, good for you.

DAPHNE. *(still a little cool)* I'm happy to hear that.

CLAIRE. Yes.

DONALD. And he – Mr. Devereaux – he knows nothing?

CLAIRE. Nothing.

DONALD. What about Gordie?

CLAIRE. Nothing. He and Mr Devereaux...they've just become very good friends.

DAPHNE. I don't want to sound as though I'm interfering, Claire, but is Gordie safe, on his own, with this man?

CLAIRE. Absolutely. *(pause)* Anway, they're not entirely on their own. Two other people from the yacht club have gone out with them.

DAPHNE. Yacht club? You're not suggesting he's out in a boat?

CLAIRE. That's how they like to fish out here.

DAPHNE. Is he wearing a life jacket?

CLAIRE. Mother! Mr. Devereaux knows what he's doing. He's Commodore of the yacht club. Top man. Very highly respected.

DONALD. *(trying to change the subject)* You say he's being cooperative?

CLAIRE. Yes. Not at first, but he's come round. Actually, it was Gordie who worked it.

DONALD. Gordie?

CLAIRE. Quite innocently. Just by being himself: always asking questions!

DAPHNE. Uh...huh.

DONALD. I know!

CLAIRE. Mr. Devereaux liked that.

DAPHNE. Why didn't you go along?

CLAIRE. Mother! What on earth are you talking about?

DAPHNE. On the fishing trip. Keep an eye on him.

CLAIRE. Actually, Mr. D asked me, but I declined.

DAPHNE. Oh, Claire! How could you...

CLAIRE. Mum: Gordie doesn't always need his mother leaning over his shoulder. It's good for him to be 'his own person.'

DONALD. *(feeling his way)* Claire: do you have an ulterior motive?

CLAIRE. How do you mean?

DONALD. Are you allowing this...this friendship...to develop so you can...say who you are? Eventually?

CLAIRE. No. Believe me, Dad. It has been spontaneous. Like it can happen sometimes.

DONALD. As long as you...

CLAIRE. No, no! I don't want to throw a monkey-wrench – a spanner – into the works.

DAPHNE. As long as you're sure Gordie's safe with him.

CLAIRE. I am, Mum. He has a wife – Helen – and she's friendly with Gordie too.

DONALD. Well, just keep it that way. If Devereaux were to find out, he might erupt – like he did with Hoogstra – and that would really upset Gordie.

DAPHNE. You know how sensitive he can be...

CLAIRE. *(wearily)* Yes, Mother. Anyway, I've got to go. They've invited me to join the three of them for a fish fry, when they come back.

DONALD. Gordie's bringing home the dinner?

CLAIRE. *(laughs)* He went out determined to haul in a salmon.

DONALD. You're in the right place for that.

CLAIRE. Sorry I woke you up. It's hard to find a 'window of opportunity' – the right moment – when you're eight hours ahead of us.

DONALD. Don't worry about it.

DAPHNE. Good night, Claire. Or should I say good afternoon?

CLAIRE. Right! Afternoon.

DAPHNE. 'Bye, dear. Give my love to Gordie. *(places phone on cradle.)*

DONALD. Mine, too. Thanks for calling, and let us know how it's going. Any time.

CLAIRE. Sure, Dad. 'Bye.

(They put down their phones; lights extinguish on **CLAIRE.** *)*

DAPHNE. I do hope she's doing the right thing. I can't say I'm happy to think of Gordie, out there on the Pacific Ocean, big waves and all that.

DONALD. It's not an ocean, my dear. It's a channel between the mainland and Vancouver Island.

DAPHNE. *(shakes head)* Just the same…

(**DONALD** *extinguishes lights, draws the curtains, and follows her to the door.*)

DONALD. Humph. It's a strange feeling, knowing that my daughter and grandson…

DAPHNE. *Our* daughter and grandson!

DONALD. Right. That they are visiting *my* father, and he and they are enjoying each other's company, yet I'm not allowed to see him. That he doesn't even acknowledge I exist.

(Lights extinguish.)

*(Lights come up on Devereaux living room. **GORDON** and **GORDIE** are sitting at a card table with three chairs pulled up to it. They are assembling a plastic Mosquito aircraft [gray plastic with a wingspan of about 22 inches]. The main frame is already assembled: fuselage, wings and tailplane. **GORDON** is dressed in casual clothing appropriate for someone who has been fishing and captains a yacht. **GORDIE** also is casually dressed and perhaps a little dishevelled. As they talk, they glue pieces together [**GORDIE** does most]. **GORDIE** is holding a piece – probably the rudder– so that when he releases it we can see it's an aircraft and he can use his hands to move it through the air. **GORDON** is holding up the tail wheel.)*

GORDON. It didn't have a tricycle landing gear, like modern planes.

GORDIE. Like a three-wheel bike?

GORDON. Exactly. Very apt. The third wheel was under the tail.

GORDIE. So you'd land like this? *(demonstrates)*

GORDON. Yes. Harder to make a smooth landing, though. You tended to float.

GORDIE. Where'd you sit?

GORDON. *(pointing to fuselage)* Here.

GORDIE. Did your navigator go down into the nose for the bombing run?

GORDON. No, no. Sat beside me all the time, on my right. But a little bit farther back. *(sees **GORDIE** is puzzled)* It's too small to see in there, Gee.

*(**GORDON** stands, pulls his chair away from the table and places it, facing downstage, in an open area toward the front of the stage.)*

Here. I'll show you. Pull that chair over, and place it beside mine: on the left.

*(**GORDIE** lays the model on the table, pulls his chair over and places it beside Gordon's.)*

GORDIE. Like this?

GORDON. Pull yours a bit farther forward…about six inches.

(**GORDIE** *adjusts position. The chairs are now 5 inches apart and the stage left chair is about six inches farther ahead than the stage right chair.*)

GORDIE. That far apart?

GORDON. Hmm – about right.

GORDIE. I mean, is there enough room for the cannon?

GORDON. You remembered it lies between us! I'm impressed, Gee.

(**GORDIE** *grins sheepishly;* **GORDON** *points to chair on left.*)

You be the pilot.

GORDIE. *(hesitates)* Shouldn't you? I mean, you were a pilot.

GORDON. I know. But today I'm along for the ride. I'll be your navigator.

GORDIE. Okay. *(sits on left seat)*

(**GORDON** *picks up 6 x 8 in. notebook from table, sits on chair on the right, places book flat on his knee.*)

GORDON. In a Mosquito, the navigator has to work on his knee. There's no room for a table. You have to imagine the cabin wall's tight against you. It's very cramped, not open like this.

(**GORDON** *pulls his arms tight in against his body.* **GORDIE** *follows suit.*)

But we've got a perspex window on each side, and over us, with an escape hatch in the roof. *(he mimes he's feeling for it)* Now, in front of us there's a control panel – air speed indicator, altimeter, gyroscope…

GORDIE. Is there a joystick?

GORDON. Yes, but it has two extensions, sideways, like a W *(double-u; demonstrates)* We call it the control column.

GORDIE. Oh. *(reaches forward and grasps imaginary handles)*

GORDON. Put your feet on the pedals *(points to imaginary pedals)*

GORDIE. Like this? *(extends his feet forward, his legs straight; they dangle in the air in front of him)*

GORDON. Right. They control the rudder. *(looks at **GORDIE**'s feet)* Hmmm.

*(**GORDON** jumps up, crosses to a footstool beside the sofa, pulls it over and pushes it in front of **GORDIE**, who lifts his feet and rests them on it.)*

There. That's better.

*(**GORDON** sits again in the navigator's chair.)*

*(During the following sequence, **GORDON** and **GORDIE** mime actions. When they climb, **GORDON** leans back and **GORDIE** follows suit. When they descend, they lean forward together. When they turn they lean to the left or right.)*

Now. When we want to climb, you pull back on the control column.

*(**GORDIE** pulls the imaginary control column quickly toward his chest.)*

Whoa, gently, or we'll flip right over....Then, when we want to descend, you push forward...

*(**GORDIE** pushes gently, smoothly forward on the control column.)*

Yes, like that...Now, to turn to the right, push gently on the right pedal and turn the wheel gently to the right...You have to do it together, to get a smooth angle of bank.

*(**GORDIE** tries it.)*

Good.

GORDIE. And do the same with the left pedal, to turn to port?

GORDON. Roger! *(surprised)* You know about port and starboard?

GORDIE. From a book. In the library.

GORDON. I see. *(slight pause)* All right, skipper! Let's start the engines. *(leans forward, pushes a button)*

(They both look to their right, at the imaginary propeller turning. We hear the sound of a Merlin inline engine starting up and running. **GORDON** *reaches forward and pushes a second button. They both look to their left at the imaginary left engine. We hear the second engine start up and run.)*

Great! Both engines running.

(Slight pause as they settle back in their seats, **GORDIE** *still holding the control column.)*

GORDIE. Are we ready for take off?

GORDON. Ready for take off! *(looks through 'perspex' to his right)* All clear starboard.

GORDIE. *(looks left)* Clear port!

GORDON. The throttles are those two knobs on the side of the cockpit, by your left knee. See them?

GORDIE. *(reaches forward with left hand)* There?

GORDON. Right.

GORDIE. Push them forward?

GORDON. Right. But slowly, sm-o-o-thly. Now release the brake – it's a button on the control column.

(After a few moments, **GORDON** *starts bouncing in his seat;* **GORDIE** *sees what he's doing, bounces too. Engine noise grows louder.)*

(In the following sequence we are aware that **GORDON** *is overcoming his fears, his wartime flying memories;* **GORDIE** *has unwittingly forced him to face something he has carefully chosen to forget.)*

We're on the take-off run. You look straight ahead, keep us on the runway. I'll watch the airspeed. At one hundred and ninety knots, pull gently back on the stick. *(mimes watching air speed indicator)*…one hundred…one hundred thirty…one seventy…Now!

(GORDIE pulls back on control column; they both lean back and stop bouncing. They are both "living" the moment; they pause at appropriate moments to scan the sky. Lights around them dim so they are both spotlighted.)

GORDON. *(cont.)* Airborne! *(pretends to write in his log – on knee)*

GORDIE. Cool! I mean, cool!!

GORDON. Turn starboard, skipper. Course one-seven-seven degrees. Climb to five thousand feet.

(They both lean back and to the right.)

GORDIE. One-seven-seven.

(They sit upright, still leaning back.)

Approaching five thousand feet.

GORDON. Ease back on the throttles and level out.

(GORDIE pulls back on throttles; they sit upright, engine noise lessens.)

Watch out for fighters.

(They search the sky.)

GORDIE. I'm searching.

GORDON. Target straight ahead, skipper. Be there in six minutes.

(Pause; they bounce along, look out of windows; suddenly, GORDON looks and points to his right, shouts:)

M.E. One O Nine! Three o'clock high!

GORDIE. *(looks to the right)* Turning starboard!…

(GORDIE pushes throttles forward – engine noise increases; they have to raise their voices to shout over the noise.)

Got him in my sights. Where's the firing button?

GORDON. On the control column. Under your left thumb.

GORDIE. Closing…

GORDON. Five hundred yards…three hundred…Fire!

GORDIE. Right!

(Presses button; sound of rapid fire; they bounce. After a moment **GORDIE** *leans to the right and peers out and downward through* **GORDON**'s *"window.")*

Wow! We got it!

GORDON. He's going down.

(They both look down to the right; pause as they watch; both are intense, absorbed.)

GORDON. Turn back to course one-six-four.

GORDIE. One-six-four.

(They lean to the left, then after a few seconds, straighten out; engine noise decreases.)

GORDON. Target directly ahead...Bomb doors open...Prepare to dive...Release bombs at one thousand feet.

*(***HELEN*** and ***CLAIRE*** enter from kitchen area, stand and watch, unnoticed. After a few moments ***HELEN*** instinctively places a hand on ***CLAIRE***'s arm, awed at what she sees ***GORDON*** doing; she's aware he's facing ghosts from his past.)*

GORDIE. Down we go! *(pushes control column forward; they lean forward)*

GORDON. *(watching altimeter)* Three thousand feet.... Hold airspeed three six zero...

GORDIE. Three six zero!

GORDON. ...twentyfive hundred...two thousand...fifteen hundred...ready?

GORDIE. Ready!

GORDON. Twelve hundred...one thousand...

GORDIE. *(pushes button on control column)* Bombs away!

GORDON. Pull up! Pull up! Turn port...

*(***GORDIE*** pulls back on control column, pushes throttles forward – engine noise increases.)*

GORDIE. *(leans back, looks to his left and down)* Wow! Right on target! A bullseye!

GORDON. Steer course three-four-six. Let's head for home.

(**GORDIE** *pulls back on throttles; engine noise decreases and dies out. Lights come up on remainder of scene.*)

HELEN. What on earth are you two doing?

GORDIE. *(excited)* Gee's showing me how to fly, like in a Mosquito!

GORDON. Exhausting work! *(pulls out handkerchief, mops brow and neck; he has been sweating, reliving a real experience)* Young Gee here would make a very good pilot. Excellent control.

(**HELEN** *has walked over to* **GORDON**, *places her hands on his shoulders; she understands that he has faced and to some extent overcome a personal problem.*)

(**GORDIE** *jumps out of chair, picks up model, runs with it to* **CLAIRE**.)

GORDIE. Look what we're making! A Mosquito Mark nineteen. Gee bought it for me.

CLAIRE. Mmmm. *(to* **GORDON***)* You're spoiling him. First the fishing. Now this!

GORDON. Well worth it.

GORDIE. *(pointing inside model)* This is where the pilot and navigator sit. It's very narrow and the entrance is a trapdoor under the navigator's feet. Isn't that right, Gee?

GORDON. Absolutely.

CLAIRE. Just a moment, Gordie. *(to* **GORDON***)* What's this 'Gee' business? You both say it!

HELEN. *(laughs)* It all started when Gee asked…I mean, when Gordie asked…if it wasn't a bit clumsy for him to keep saying 'Mr. Devereaux'…

GORDON. So I suggested he call me 'Gee'…

HELEN. We felt 'Uncle Gordon' would be too formal…old fashioned…

GORDON. And then Gordie said 'But I'm a Gee, too."…

HELEN. We laughed at that…

GORDIE. So we decided he'd be 'Big Gee' and I'd be 'Little Gee'...

GORDON. But only till he has grown taller than me...

GORDIE. Then I'll be 'Big Gee'!

GORDON. *(laughs)* And I'll be 'Little Gee'...In about five, six years, perhaps...

CLAIRE. *(to* **HELEN***)* Have you become 'H'?

GORDIE. Like we're working our way through the alphabet?

HELEN. No. We decided I'd be 'Mrs. Gee.'

CLAIRE. Wouldn't 'Mrs D.' be more logical?

HELEN. Oh, no. Too formal. *(to* **GORDON***)* Okay, Big Gee: I need you to light the barbecue.

GORDON. Right! *(to* **CLAIRE***; as* **GORDON** *walks through French window)* You're going to savour young Gee's catch.

GORDIE. Two, Mum! Big salmon *(spreads his arms)* And Big Gee caught one too *(smaller arm spread).*

HELEN. *(to* **GORDON***)* I've seasoned them and wrapped them in foil. *(to* **CLAIRE***)* Gordon cooks them whole on the barbecue. It's his specialty.

(**GORDIE** *puts the model on the table, then chases after* **GORDON***, out through the French windows. As they converse,* **HELEN** *pushes chairs back to their original positions and examines model.)*

CLAIRE. I really don't know how to thank you and Mr. Devereaux...

HELEN. Oh, my dear: the pleasure has been all ours. Your son...he's been so good for Gordon. He's come right out of himself.

CLAIRE. I would have said it's the other way round.

HELEN. Oh, no. Even when our granddaughters visit – which isn't all that often, now their parents have moved to California – they aren't interested in doing things with him. They think we're a couple of old fogies. They're older than Gordie – teen agers – just old enough to think we're beyond it.

(They exit toward kitchen. Lights extinguish.)

(Lights up on Barlow living room, early morning; cur-
tains are drawn, room is semi-dark. Enter **DONALD***;*
opens curtains, sunlight streams through windows.
Phone rings. **DONALD** *picks up portable phone.)*

DONALD. Five two eight seven one two....

(Lights up on **CLAIRE***, on motel phone, sitting on bed,*
dressed as in previous scene. Speaks quietly, because
GORDIE *is asleep in another part of room.)*

CLAIRE. Dad: It's Claire.

DONALD. Oh! Hello, Claire! *(looks at clock)* My goodness!
What time is it there?

CLAIRE. Eleven-fifty-five. Night.

DONALD. It's seven-fifty-five here. Morning.

CLAIRE. Can you hear me all right?

DONALD. Yes, I think so. A little quiet perhaps.

CLAIRE. *(glances sideways offstage, to check)* Gordie's asleep. I
don't want to disturb him.

DONALD. He's all right?

CLAIRE. Fine. In fact, he's had a marvelous day.

DONALD. Do I need to call your mother?

CLAIRE. No. This is...*(about you.)*

DONALD. It took her awhile to get to sleep last night.

CLAIRE. No. Leave her. I'm sorry about the late call.

DONALD. So, what's happened? For you to call us again so
soon?

CLAIRE. I think this might be an appropriate moment for
you to fly out here.

DONALD. You mean, Devereaux knows...?

CLAIRE. No.

DONALD. ...and accepts?

CLAIRE. No.

DONALD. Then...?

CLAIRE. Something extraordinary has happened. He and
Gordie were role-playing they were flying together
and – I don't quite know how to explain it – somehow

Gordon – Mr. Devereaux...It was as though he broke through a barrier – could look at his past without fear and trembling. And Gordie did it with him – like a catalyst. *(slight pause)* They've become such great pals, Dad. It's like a miracle. Even Helen – Mrs. Devereaux – she says so...I've never seen anything like it. *(pause)* Are you there?

DONALD. Yes, I'm listening. Claire: I don't think it would be wise. I wouldn't want to break in – burst the bubble, so to speak.

CLAIRE. I don't think...*(it would...)*

DONALD. *(interrupts)* To protect Gordie, more than Devereaux.

CLAIRE. I think she knows – his wife, Helen. Or at least suspects. Something she said to me afterward...It's hard to pin down...And her manner to me: positive, almost supportive. It was subliminal, but it *was* there.

*(**DAPHNE** walks in bearing early morning tea on tray.)*

DONALD. Oh, I don't know, Claire.

CLAIRE. Dad, I think you should.

DONALD. You mean, risk it?

CLAIRE. No. Try. It's like a tiny little window has opened. You won't have another chance.

*(**DONALD** signals to **DAPHNE** to silently pick up the phone.)*

DONALD. My inclination is to say: 'Yes. Grab it.' But my commonsense is saying: 'Be sensible; be cautious.'

CLAIRE. *(rattled)* Stop acting like a banker, Dad. I'm not asking you for a loan! *(pause)* Look: in three days Gordie and I will be driving away from Vancouver; from Gordon and Helen. We'll say goodbye to them, and probably never see them again. I'm sure, before we leave, they'll invite us to visit again, and Gordie and I will promise to do so, but they'll know in their hearts – and I will too – that it won't happen. Time and natural drift will eat away at our promises.

DONALD. But won't Gordie expect it to happen?

CLAIRE. Yes. And the only way it *can* happen is for you to come and open the door for us: cement the relationship.

DONALD. Or Devereaux will slam the door shut, noisily and permanently.

CLAIRE. That's a risk we have to take.

DONALD. What about Gordie? How will he feel if he...

CLAIRE. *(interrupts)* I don't think Mr. Devereaux would say or do anything to hurt Gordie. To me, maybe. But not to Gordie.

(long pause)

DONALD. Can you give me twenty-four hours? To think about it?

CLAIRE. No, Dad. You need to fly out tonight. Tomorrow at the latest. Arrive tomorrow night.

(pause)

DONALD. *(suddenly decisive)* I'll call you back in half an hour. What's your number?

CLAIRE. No, Dad. I'll call you. The phone ring might wake Gordie. Half past twelve my time.

DONALD. Eight-thirty mine.

CLAIRE. Dad: this is the only chance you'll have...

DONALD. *(interrupts)* Claire! Stop! Just call me in half an hour.

CLAIRE. *(surprised at his tone)* Right, Dad. *(She hangs up phone, almost in tears, looks at where* GORDIE *sleeps off stage.)* This is for you, Gordie.

(Lights extinguish over motel bedroom.)

*(*DONALD *switches off phone, lays it down;* DAPHNE *replaces phone on cradle.)*

DAPHNE. So: another decision!

DONALD. What do you think, Daph?

DAPHNE. Oh, no. You have to make that decision. And fast.

DONALD. Oh, lord. Of course I want to go. But I don't want to risk a flare-up; upset Gordie.

DAPHNE. Understandable. *(She has pre-thought this.)* Have you considered going as Claire's father-in-law? As Donald Summers rather than Donald Barlow?

DONALD. *(he doesn't like idea)* What?!

DAPHNE. Clear it with Claire first.

> *(**DONALD** shakes head, bewildered.)*

Then you'd meet him, see him, without any risk of…

DONALD. *(interrupts)* Without risk?! It'd be much too dangerous. Gordie would know. He'd ask questions; spill the beans.

DAPHNE. Claire could prepare him; tell him in advance. Explain why.

DONALD. You can't put a load like that on a nine-year-old! Anyway, Gordie's to know the connection *only* if everything works out. Then his relationship to Devereaux will strengthen. Not be shattered.

DAPHNE. So go as yourself. When you arrive, get some sort of 'sense' from Claire as to whether you're to go to the house.

DONALD. You're saying I should go, then?

DAPHNE. No. I'm just trying to be objective, see all the angles.

> *(Slight pause. **DONALD** looks at his watch, strides impatiently, his back to **DAPHNE**.)*

> *(matter-of-factly)* Both British Airways and Air Canada fly daily to Vancouver from Heathrow; direct flights; leave about noon; arrive the same day – mid to late afternoon.

> *(**DONALD** looks at her in amazement.)*

I looked it up on the internet, just in case.

DONALD. Good lord. But I'd never make it today.

DAPHNE. Tomorrow would be fine. You'll be flying with the sun.

DONALD. You'll come too? *(He expects her to.)*

DAPHNE. No. *(slight pause)* Two reasons: we can't afford it…

DONALD. Sure we can…

DAPHNE. *(raises her hand to stop him)* It'll be a last-minute booking – no discount…

    (DONALD *goes to argue; she still restrains him.)*

This is something *you* need to do. For yourself…for your mother.

DONALD. *(thoughtfully)* And for young Gordie. *(sighs)* Yes.

DAPHNE. And, perhaps, for your father. *(She gives* **DONALD** *a hug.)*

    (Lights extinguish.)

(Lights come up on Devereaux living room. **GORDON** *and* **GORDIE** *walk in from kitchen area, carrying items of* **GORDON**'s *uniform:* **GORDON** *carries a tissue-wrapped package that contains his officer's jacket [RCAF]; it has squadron leader stripes, pilot's wings, three medal ribbons [DFC, Canadian war medal, etc], and a pathfinder's badge beneath them in the middle of the left pocket;* **GORDIE** *wears* **GORDON**'s *flat, rather worn RCAF officer's cap perched loosely on his head – but he is proud of it.* **GORDIE** *also carries the now-nearly-finished model Mosquito, which still needs air force roundels [decals] to be inserted on wings and fuselage. In an aged envelope* **GORDON** *has his flying log. They place the items on the table.)*

GORDON. I flew with the Canadian air force most of the time, but late in 1944 I was seconded to an R.A.F. squadron.

GORDIE. Seconded?

GORDON. Hmmm: Sent there on loan, for three months in my case. My navigator and me.

GORDIE. Is that when you flew that special operation: the raid on a prison in Belgium.

GORDON. Gee: you never cease to surprise me!

GORDIE. Mummy told me about it. That's what she's writing about, isn't it?

GORDON. Sort of. Not so much about the flying – the operation – but about the pilots and navigators who flew it, and what they are doing now.

GORDIE. Like fishing in the Pacific Ocean.

GORDON. The Georgia Strait.

GORDIE. *(nods in agreement)* And building model aeroplanes.

GORDON. *(laughs)* Just when you're here! Now, let's see… *(He unwraps tissue from uniform, pulls on the uniform jacket, which is a tight fit and won't button across the front.)* Oh, my goodness!

GORDIE. Phew! It smells.

GORDON. Moth balls. Mrs. Gee put them in the pockets. See: no holes!

GORDIE. *(reaches up to medal ribbons)* These are your flying medals?

GORDON. Right.

GORDON. What's this one for?

GORDON. Canadian War Service. The maple leaf in the middle means I served overseas.

GORDIE. *(moves hand to next medal)* This one?

GORDON. DFC. *(sees question on **GORDIE**'s face; reluctantly)* Distinguished Flying Cross.

GORDIE. Wow! You received the DFC? C-o-o-l! You must have been very brave! *(moves hand to badge in middle of breast pocket, below wings)* For when you were a Pathfinder?

GORDON. How did you know about Pathfinders?

GORDIE. Mr. Waggoner told me. He was one too.

GORDON. Yes. He would.

GORDIE. What did a Pathfinder do?

GORDON. Flew over the target ahead of the bombers – low down. Dropped flares over the target – very bright lights – for the bombers, high-up, to aim at.

GORDIE. *(impressed)* I wish I could have done flying like that.

GORDON. Not as glamorous as it may seem, Gee. *(He starts taking off jacket.)*

GORDIE. Were you scared?

GORDON. *(simply)* Yes. Often.

*(**GORDIE** senses not to pursue topic; he runs over to a mirror on one of the walls, above his eye level, pulls a chair over to it, kicks off his shoes, climbs onto chair and inspects himself in the mirror.)*

GORDIE. I wish my grandpa could see me like this!

GORDON. Not your dad?

GORDIE. Nah! I don't think he'd be interested. Now if I was wearing a hockey helmet and mask, then he would.

GORDON. *(laughs)* Like Gordie Howe!

GORDIE. You bet. *(looks at himself in hat)* But my grandpa would like to see this.

GORDON. You have just one grandpa?

GORDIE. No. Two. But the other one lives in Cornwall. I don't see him much.

GORDON. That's your mother's dad?

GORDIE. No, my dad's. Grandpa Summers.

GORDON. Oh, I see.

> **(GORDIE** *jumps down from chair. Pushes it back in place, crosses to table, points to package.)*

GORDIE. What's in there?

GORDON. My pilot's log.

GORDIE. Can I see it?

GORDON. Sure. *(He unwraps logbook, opens it, points to it.)* You write down every flight you take: the date, type of aircraft, take-off time, length of flight, things like that.

GORDIE. Your writing wasn't very good.

GORDON. No. Now, if I'd been a navigator, and had to keep a detailed record of each flight…

GORDIE. Then you'd have been neater?

GORDON. *(laughs)* I guess I'd have had to be. *(flips to a different page)*

GORDIE. *(reads)* Twenty-eighth of August, 1943. Mosquito three four six. Air Sea Firing. Navigator John Webster. Two hours zero seven minutes.

GORDON. I was at Debert, then, in Nova Scotia; O.C.U.

GORDIE. O.C.U.?

GORDON. Operational Conversion Unit. Where we crewed up, before going overseas; learned how to fly on operations.

GORDIE. *(flips to another page; reads)* 14th March 1944. Mosquito two seven one. Ferry aircraft Scampton to Waddington. *(looks up at* **GORDON***)* Those air bases are near Lincoln, aren't they? One on each side.

GORDON. How did you know that?

GORDIE. My Nan lived there. In Lincoln.

GORDON. Your Nan?

GORDIE. My grandpa's mum. That's where my grandpa lived, before he moved to Nottingham.

GORDON. Which grandpa was that?

GORDIE. Grandpa Don.

GORDON. Sorry. I'm confused...

GORDIE. My mum's Dad.

GORDON. *(very cautiously)* And...his name is...

GORDIE. Don...Donald.

GORDON. Donald...Summers?

GORDIE. No. *(He's bored with this conversation.)* Donald Barlow.

(GORDON freezes, tries to stay calm.)

GORDON. Do you...er...have any great-grandparents now?

GORDIE. No. I did. But she died. *(turns pages)* Where's the raid my Mum's writing about?

GORDON. *(flips pages; he's uptight now)* Did your...great-grandmother...your Dad's mom...did she live in Lincoln too?

GORDIE. Oh, yes. She's buried there. Up near the cathedral.

GORDON. *(points to an entry)* There. And her name was...?

GORDIE. *(bored by question)* Mrs. Barlow.

GORDON. No. Her first name?

GORDIE. Umm...*(tries to remember)*...Gladys...no, that was my other grandmother's mother...she lived in Shrewsbury. *(pause)* Does Wendy sound right?

GORDON. *(with great control)* I have no idea, Gee.

(GORDON paces over to French window, peers out, highly perturbed.)

GORDIE. I think that's right: Wendy.

(GORDON marches to kitchen door, opens it.)

GORDON. *(bellows)* Helen. Can you come here a minute?

(**GORDON** *slams door shut, marches back to window, stares out.* **GORDIE** *is puzzled by his actions, knows it's better not to say anything. Enter* **HELEN**.)

HELEN. You called, dear?

GORDON. *(trying to stay calm; pointedly)* Can you find a coke for Gordie here. I need to talk some more with Mrs. Summers.

(*Both* **HELEN** *and* **GORDIE** *are surprised at his demeanour and formality.*

HELEN. *(looks at watch; to* **GORDIE**) More than a coke, I think. Time for a snack?

GORDIE. Oh, yes, please.

(*As* **HELEN** *and* **GORDIE** *pass him,* **GORDON** *steps behind* **GORDIE** *and reaches to remove the cap. Then he thinks better of it, withdraws his hand and turns toward window. As* **HELEN** *and* **GORDIE** *reach the door, almost intuitively* **GORDIE** *turns around, takes off the cap, and runs back with it to* **GORDON**.

GORDIE. Thank you for letting me wear your cap.

GORDON. *(nonplussed)* Oh – uh – it was my pleasure. *(slight pause)* It suits you.

(**GORDIE** *grins and skips back toward door, picks up his shoes and carries them out.*)

(to **HELEN***; curtly)* Ask Mrs. Summers to join me, will you?

(**HELEN** *and* **GORDIE** *exit.* **GORDON** *carries cap back toward table, picks up logbook and snaps it shut, replaces it in envelope, and lays it on the table with the cap on top of it. Picks up uniform jacket, folds it inside out so the insignia cannot be seen, and carefully lays it on top of the hat and log, so it conceals them.*)

(**CLAIRE** *enters:* **GORDON** *points to a chair.*)

GORDON. *(cont.) (curtly)* Sit, will you?

*(CLAIRE looks surprised at his curtness. He walks to the
window, stares out, then suddenly turns back, rests his
hands on a chairback, and leans toward her.)*

Ms. Summers.... Or should I say Miss Barlow?

*(CLAIRE looks at him in awe, as she realizes the balloon
has burst.)*

CLAIRE. How did you...? I don't know what...*(to say)*

GORDON. *(thunders it out)* Or should I say 'Grand-daughter'?

CLAIRE. I would have preferred – I planned – to stay incognito....

GORDON. You don't expect me to believe that?!

CLAIRE. I intended just to hold the interview and then leave.

GORDON. You set the whole thing up: the research...the project...just so you could...

CLAIRE. No. No....

GORDON. And you brought that boy out there along with you to soften me up; prepare the ground.

CLAIRE. No. It was never...*(She stands up, ready to leave.)*

GORDON. *(thunders it out)* **Sit down!**

CLAIRE. *(a brief pause)* I certainly will not!

*(They glare at each other. Pause. CLAIRE takes a step
toward the door.)*

GORDON. I haven't finished yet!

CLAIRE. Well, I have.

GORDON. You put me through all this, and then just...walk out?

CLAIRE. You started it!

GORDON. Oh, no. Oh, no. All that subterfuge...the duplicity...

CLAIRE. I had *no* ulterior motive...

GORDON. And you primed your son to suck me in!

CLAIRE. No. No! No! No! He knows nothing. Nothing. He is – and has been – totally innocent...

GORDON. You expect me to believe a word...

CLAIRE. ...and I don't want his innocence destroyed.

GORDON. ...after all your conniving?

CLAIRE. Yes. For my Gordie's sake, I ask you to...

GORDON. *(suddenly aware)* Gordie...Gordon...Why didn't I see it before? You named him after me! All along you've known, you've planned....

CLAIRE. That is not true! Gordie was named by his father – and it wasn't my preference...

GORDON. Oh, come now, Ms. Summers!

CLAIRE. No. No. His father is a hockey fanatic and his hero is...was...Gordie Howe. Your famous *Canadian* player. He's absolutely obsessed by him.

GORDON. You don't expect me to believe that!

CLAIRE. Gordie's birth certificate lists him as Gordie *Howe* Summers. Can you believe that?! *(sudden thought: fumbles in purse).* Here! Look at his passport! *(shoves it in front of* **GORDON***)*

GORDON. I don't need...

CLAIRE. *Look...at...it!* Read it!

GORDON. All right. All right. *(takes passport, briefly glances at it, goes to hand it back, then looks at it again – his temper is easing)* That boy is my great-grandson?

CLAIRE. *(meekly)* Yes.

(After a brief pause, he hands the passport back to **CLAIRE.***)*

You'll exclude him from any...recriminations?

GORDON. My dear woman, do you need to ask...?

CLAIRE. Then I shall say good-bye. I appreciate all you have done for Gordie. I don't appreciate the scene today. *(She is on the verge of tears, but determined to control it.)*

GORDON. Hmmph! Wait here. *(He goes to the kitchen door, calls.)* Helen! *(turns to* **CLAIRE***)* My wife will see you out.

*(***GORDON*** exits through French window. Slight pause.* **HELEN** *enters from kitchen area.)*

HELEN. *(approaching* **CLAIRE,** *with empathy)* Oh, my dear.

CLAIRE. Where is he? Gordie?

HELEN. In the study. Playing a video game.

CLAIRE. Did he hear anything?

HELEN. No. I shut the door, turned up the radio.

CLAIRE. Thank you…But you did?

HELEN. Inevitably.

CLAIRE. I'm sorry. I didn't want it to end this way.

HELEN. *(puts hand on* **CLAIRE***'s arm)* Does it have to?

CLAIRE. I've already said goodbye.

HELEN. *(softly)* For the moment.

CLAIRE. Oh, no. There's no going back…*(takes step toward farther door)* I must get Gordie.

HELEN. Do you need to?

CLAIRE. I have to. There's no way I can leave him here.

HELEN. Please! Leave him with me for a while. At least until you have calmed down. Do you want him to see you in this state?

CLAIRE. I can handle it.

HELEN. Can he? How are you going to explain your sudden anger? That you're taking him away, without explanation? Without good-byes?

CLAIRE. *(almost bubbling)* Helen…I don't understand…after all that has happened…you're still talking to me… civilly.

HELEN. My dear! I know more than you, and Gordon – particularly Gordon – more than you realize.

*(***CLAIRE*** sinks into a chair, unable to grasp what she hears.)*

The first day you were here. I took Gordie into the kitchen – remember? – while you and Gordon talked. We were sitting at the table and Gordie said: "You're like my Grannie Barlow. She let's me have Coca Cola too. My mum doesn't approve." *(***HELEN*** laughs; slight pause.)* I'd heard the name Barlow before.

CLAIRE. You never said anything.

HELEN. No. There was no point. And I might have been mistaken.

CLAIRE. And you didn't mention it to Mr. Devereaux?

HELEN. To Gordon? No. He wouldn't have listened. He'd have sent you packing, right away. I felt…I wanted… to trust you.

(**CLAIRE** *shakes head in wonder and admiration.*)

Then, when I saw how well Gordon and Gordie were getting along…*(laughs)* The two 'Gees'…I couldn't… *(slight pause)* Were you planning to tell Gordon?

CLAIRE. No. It was to be only an interview. Then we'd leave. No more than that. But…as you and Mr. Devereaux gradually drew us into your little circle, my resolve…

HELEN. Slipped?

(**CLAIRE** *nods.*)

I so admire your dedication. Your strength.

CLAIRE. You won't now.

(*Pause;* **HELEN** *looks questioningly at* **CLAIRE.**)

I phoned my father. He arrives this afternoon.

HELEN. Hmmm. That *will* be interesting.

CLAIRE. I thought that the atmosphere had developed to a point where…the moment was…*(shrugs, searching for a word)*

HELEN. Propitious?

CLAIRE. *(nods)* How wrong I was!

HELEN. *(thoughtfully)* Not necessarily.

CLAIRE. I'll tell him to turn round – fly home.

HELEN. No, no. Let me talk to Gordon.

CLAIRE. There's no point; he's so adamant.

HELEN. Let me try.

CLAIRE. *(shrugs)* What about Gordie?

HELEN. Leave him with me. I'll drive him down to your motel later. I'll phone you first.

(*CLAIRE turns to exit.* HELEN *gives her a quick hug, which almost triggers more tears.*)

CLAIRE. I can find my way out.

(*CLAIRE exits.* HELEN *brushes her hands together [as though dusting off chalk], then walks resolutely to the French window.*)

HELEN. (*calls upstage*) Gordon.

(*Slight pause;* GORDON *enters tentatively, looks around.*)

GORDON. Has she gone?

HELEN. Yes.

GORDON. Taken the boy with her?

HELEN. No.

GORDON. He's still here?

HELEN. She was in no state to...

GORDON. (*reluctantly agreeing with her*) No. (*pause*) Where is he?

HELEN. On my computer. He'll be a while. (*pause*) Why are you so against meeting her father?

GORDON. (*appalled*) You know? She told you about him? That woman...!

HELEN. No, Gordon. She has said nothing. I knew before.

GORDON. You *couldn't* have known!

HELEN. I made enquiries.

GORDON. You went behind my back?

HELEN. Behind your back? No more than you...(*shrugs; slight pause*) Six months ago – about that – you had a visit from a man from the Netherlands...

GORDON. Hoogstra.

HELEN. You were very angry with him. Unreasonably so, I thought. (*pause*) He left his card: Connexion Closure. I phoned him.

GORDON. That was private!

HELEN. From your wife?

GORDON. But he told me his information was confidential!

HELEN. From me, Gordon? *(pause)* I talked to him, squeezed a name from him: Wendy Barlow.

GORDON. That was before your time!

HELEN. Were you trying to conceal something?

GORDON. I don't want to talk about it.

HELEN. Something you didn't want me to know?

GORDON. *(with extreme emphasis)* I don't want to talk about it!

HELEN. But why?

GORDON. Helen. I knew nothing about…what happened to her. About her…child…son. *Nothing!*

HELEN. Until that man came barging in? *(he nods)* Why didn't you tell me? Share it with me?

GORDON. I…I was afraid you'd be upset…angry. *(reluctantly)* You wouldn't like knowing there was someone before you.

HELEN. Someone you slept with?

(He nods, abashed.)

Oh, Gordon! If this was nineteen-forty-five, yes, I probably would have been upset. Very! *(slight pause)* But today, young people think very little of it. They'd be the exception if they did. Look at our daughters! Both have lived with more than one man, before they married.

(pause)

GORDON. How long have you known?

HELEN. About Wendy Barlow? Quite some time.

GORDON. And her son?

HELEN. The same.

GORDON. You didn't say anything!

HELEN. No.

GORDON. Why ever not?

HELEN. I guess, because I didn't want to upset you.

GORDON. Any more than I wanted to upset you.

(She hugs him. He is a bit easier with himself.)

HELEN. Were you...Did you love her?

GORDON. *(after a painful pause; with difficulty)* I don't know, Helen. I really don't...I think...perhaps I thought I was...It was so long ago...*(pause)* Oh, I was so...Terrified.... Night after night...searchlights probing for us... flak sliding up toward us, from guns on the ground... bursting around us...bombs falling from the hundreds of bombers high above us, as we flew in and out, over the target, directing their aim...I was so afraid their bombs would fall on us...Lancasters...in flames...rolling down past us.... *(pause)* Then the weather would break...there'd be a stand-down. We'd take a train into London. Many flyers would head for a pub, to escape their fear....I'd walk the streets, help where I could, see homes with just one wall left, furniture protruding from it...search in piles of rubble...whole families buried... *(slight pause: he finds this memory difficult)* One morning...oh, a dreadful morning...I was shoving bricks and rubble aside, when I unearthed the arm of a young girl, no more than six or seven, a doll still clutched in her hand. *(slight pause)* After that, I didn't want to fly any more: guide our bombers to annihilate families in Germany...Had to *drive* myself to do it.

(pause)

I couldn't face going into London again...I'd take a local bus into Lincoln, to a *private home*...where they didn't ask questions...they just seemed to *understand.*And Wendy was there...For a few hours I could forget....

*(**HELEN** holds her arms around him.)*

HELEN. Oh, my man. You never told me....

GORDON. I couldn't. I just couldn't.

*(**HELEN** holds him even tighter to her.)*

HELEN. Have you told Claire, what it was like? The flying?

GORDON. No; not like that. No one. Ever....

HELEN. I think you should, if only so she could understand you better.

GORDON. Her? Not likely!

HELEN. I wish you'd try. *(slight pause)* Don't you like the idea of having a great-grandson?

GORDON. It makes me sound...so old.

HELEN. Oh, not you!

GORDON. *(slight smile)* I suppose, if I were to choose a great-grandson...

HELEN. It would be a boy like Little Gee?

GORDON. *(smiles)* Let's go and see what he's doing.

(**GORDON** *pulls cap out from under his jacket. They walk toward the door to the kitchen.*)

HELEN. Of course, there's a corollary...

GORDON. There always is, Helen, with you.

HELEN. *(she laughs lightly)* You realize, don't you, that you can't have a great-grandson without first having a grandson or a granddaughter? And, before that, a son or a daughter?

(Lights extinguish.)

(Lights come up on **DONALD** *and* **CLAIRE** *in a corner of the motel bedroom. It is three hours later.* **DONALD** *sits in the chair;* **CLAIRE** *sits on the bed. Small side table between them, with telephone on it.)*

DONALD. I didn't entirely believe Paul Hoogstra when he said Devereaux was brutal. From what you say, it's true.

CLAIRE. He was *so* angry. Vicious.

DONALD. Your mother was right. I should never have come.

CLAIRE. I'm sorry, Dad. I shouldn't have…

DONALD. Nonsense. It was my decision. You're sure you should've left Gordie with them?

CLAIRE. Absolutely. Helen…Mrs Devereaux…it was her idea. She'll bring him round later, so I don't have to go back there. *(sees* **DONALD** *'s hesitation)* No. He won't touch Gordie. On that score, if no other, I trust him.

(slight pause)

DONALD. Does Gordie know I'm here?

CLAIRE. No. It'll be a surprise. And he knows nothing about my argument with Devereaux.

DONALD. Does he know…?

CLAIRE. That Devereaux's his great-grandfather? *(***DONALD** *nods.)* No.

(Pause.)

What will you do now?

DONALD. Sleep first. *(looks at watch)* My body tells me it's one a.m. Then tomorrow I'll call Air Canada.

CLAIRE. Do you have to fly home right away? You could drive with Gordie and me to Calgary – through the Rockie Mountains – then fly home from there.

DONALD. It's a thought.

CLAIRE. My last interview is at Kelowna, in between two mountain ranges.

DONALD. Let me sleep on it. Then I'll call your mother.

CLAIRE. She'll say 'yes,' I'm sure.

(Telephone rings.)

DONALD. *(laughs)* That'll be her! Checking I got here all right.

*(**CLAIRE** picks up phone.)*

CLAIRE. Hello?...Oh, it's you, Helen...Yes, he's here...You want us to come there?...Now? *(slight laugh)* I doubt whether he'll agree...All right. If you don't here from me within ten minutes, know we'll be coming. *(puts down phone)* Helen Devereaux...

DONALD. So I gathered.

CLAIRE. She wants me to take you up there.

DONALD. You've got to be joking!

CLAIRE. No. She's dead serious.

DONALD. Absolutely not. Out of the question.

CLAIRE. She said he's calmed down. I suspect *she* calmed him down. Her exact words were: 'I think you should strike while the iron is hot.'

DONALD. Too hot! Much too hot.

CLAIRE. Dad: you should. You've come this far....

DONALD. No way. I want nothing to do with him.

CLAIRE. You're giving up?

DONALD. You can't expect me to...

CLAIRE. What have you got to lose?

DONALD. My dignity. Maybe my teeth.

CLAIRE. Dad...

DONALD. After how he treated you?

CLAIRE. I think now, perhaps it was partly my fault. I let it drift too long. If I'd said something earlier...been up front with him...it would have been less of a surprise.

DONALD. Come, Claire! Be realistic. He would have been just the same....

CLAIRE. Dad: I've got to know this man. And so has Gordie...

*(**DONALD** goes to remonstrate; **CLAIRE** raises her hand
to halt him.)*

Let me finish. Gordie thinks the world of him. And he
of Gordie. Regardless of how you and I feel personally,
I think we should try. *(looks at watch).* Come on!

*(She takes **DONALD**'s hand, pulls; he rises reluctantly.)*

(Lights extinguish as they exit.)

(Lights come up on the Devereaux living room. **HELEN**
is arranging flowers in a vase. **GORDON** *enters through
French windows.)*

GORDON. Gee's nearly about finished the Mosquito: just
got to stick the roundels on the wings and fuselage.

HELEN. When did *you* last build a model like that?

GORDON. *(laughs)* Before the war. But it wasn't plastic. Balsa
wood. It was supposed to fly.

HELEN. Did it?

GORDON. Once. I couldn't face rebuilding it!

HELEN. Gordie's done a good job on his.

GORDON. For a nine-year-old, yes.

HELEN. For a seventy-five-year-old helper, also yes. *(pause)*
Claire's coming to pick him up. Very shortly.

GORDON. I don't want to see her.

HELEN. That's up to you.

GORDON. No. Definitely not.

HELEN. Is Gordie to take the model with him?

GORDON. Of course.

HELEN. And your cap?

GORDON. *(slight pause)* No. I'd rather not. Knowing where
it will go.

HELEN. *(after a pause; carefully)* How do you feel…? Um…
Am I to ask them to visit again? They have two more
days in Vancouver.

GORDON. Ugh! *(pause)* I would have liked to take Gordie
fishing again. No way now.

HELEN. Why not? *(slight pause)* You'd rather not see his
mother?

GORDON. *(pause)* Right.

HELEN. It's a stumbling block? *(he nods)* Why?

GORDON. She made a fool of me.

HELEN. Or did you make a fool of yourself?

GORDON. Helen! Can we drop it?

HELEN. No. What do you *really* think: Did Claire come here just to get a story from you? Or was her real reason to identify herself as your granddaughter and her father as your son?

GORDON. Please, Helen! Can we...?

HELEN. No. I want to deal with it!

(GORDON sighs, sits.)

Did Claire take any steps to identify herself? To confront you?

GORDON. No. But there was still time.

HELEN. Do you believe she primed Gordie? Set him up.

GORDON. No. Not now...But...

HELEN. Then, Gordon, why are you so angry with her?

(He throws his arms up helplessly. She goes up to him.)

Your ego has been bruised, hasn't it?

GORDON. Helen: how can I possibly face her, after all that was said?

HELEN. Do you think, perhaps, she might welcome it?

GORDON. No, I don't.

HELEN. That you are trying to clear the air...?

(GORDON shakes head 'no.')

That she'll be a lot more comfortable with us, now everything's out in the open?

GORDON. Possibly.

HELEN. That she won't feel like she's walking on hot bricks any more?

GORDON. *(after a brief pause; suddenly)* You like her, don't you?

HELEN. Yes, I do. I like her guts. She's a strong woman. And that's one of the difficulties: you're a strong man.

GORDON. All right, all right. But how...?

HELEN. Just by going up to her and saying: "Can we start again?"

GORDON. Just like that?

HELEN. Sure. And I'll wager she'll say: "Yes, let's."

GORDON. You make it sound so...easy.

HELEN. Yes, well...You'll do it?

GORDON. For you, yes.

HELEN. No! For you.

GORDON. All right.

HELEN. And for Gordie?

GORDON. I'll ask him if he wants to go fishing tomorrow.

HELEN. Oh, he will!

> (**GORDON** *walks toward French windows. She intercepts him, places a hand on his arm.*)

There is...one more thing you need to know.

> (**GORDON** *looks suspiciously at her.*)

Claire is not driving up here alone.

GORDON. Are you telling me....?

HELEN. Her father is here.

GORDON. That two-faced, scheming woman! She knew all along...

HELEN. *(firmly)* All right! He will stay in the car. He doesn't want to come in any more than you want him here.

GORDON. *(angry)* Helen: How involved are you in all this?

HELEN. Sit down. Sit down! You're the one who's making all the noise, but – think about it – I'm the one who should, perhaps, be most incensed!

GORDON. Then why aren't you?

HELEN. Because...Because I have come to terms with it; I can see both sides. At first, when I...intuited...there had been someone before me...but you never mentioned her, or that there was a child...

GORDON. I didn't know there was a child!

HELEN. Granted. I was so *angry*, Gordon!

GORDON. *(slight pause)* Is that when you went off in such a hurry, to see your sister in Montreal?

HELEN. *(nods; pause)* But, gradually, as she and I talked

– and we did talk! – she helped me see that no one had been trying to conceal anything from me; there was no reason for me to be angry with anyone.

(**GORDON** *looks strangely at her.*)

(gently, with understanding) You never knew that... Wendy...had a child?

GORDON. No. I never saw her again. My kitbag was stolen when I was in the Pacific; her address was in it.

HELEN. *(wryly)* From my point of view, how very fortunate.

(He walks up to her, places an arm around her shoulders.)

After the war, you never tried to find her?

GORDON. No. I thought about it, but...so much was happening, and international travel wasn't as simple then, as it is now. I wasn't demobilized until December; went straight into the family business, and then on to university...where I met you.

HELEN. I love you, and I don't want the discomfort you are feeling to continue.

(She hugs him. Sound of doorbell. She stands back from him, looks at him, steps forward and hugs him again. Walks toward hall door.)

GORDON. *(it's an appeal)* Helen...

HELEN. *(hand on door handle)* If he chooses to come in, I'll send him in to you right away, but on his own. I suggest you stand over there *(points to area opposite the kitchen door)*. If, when you see him, you don't want to continue, just turn your back, face the kitchen. You need not say anything. I'll tell him, so he'll know to turn around himself and come back out. All right?

*(**GORDON** nods, shakes his head miserably. **HELEN** turns to exit.)*

GORDON. *(another appeal)* Helen...?

*(**HELEN** pauses, looks at him firmly.)*

HELEN. I'll go and find Gordie.

*(She turns away and exits into hall. **GORDON** walks to French window, makes as if he is about to exit through it [i.e. escape], thinks better of it, turns and stands in area facing across from the kitchen door.)*

(There are voices from offstage:)

DONALD. *(voice over)* Claire: This is *not* a good idea.

CLAIRE. *(voice over)* Dad! Don't back out now! Please! All you have to do is step in, acknowledge he's there. If he acknowledges you, fine! Continue. If he doesn't, just do as Helen said: turn round and come out.

*(Pause. **DONALD** enters without looking up, pulls door shut behind him, turns, stands stationary, looks up at **GORDON**.)*

*(**GORDON** stands silent, watching.)*

(pause)

DONALD. *(slowly)* Hello, father.

(pause)

GORDON. Son.

*(Pause. **GORDON** starts to turn as though he is about to break off the meeting. Seeing this, **DONALD** turns too, toward hall door, as if about to exit. At that moment **GORDIE** enters through French window. He's wearing **GORDON**'s cap and is holding the completed model aloft, 'flying' it. **GORDIE** pauses when he sees **GORDON** turning away, senses a second person's presence, looks to his left, sees his grandfather. Neither man has noticed he's there.)*

GORDIE. *(surprised; overjoyed; staying where he is)* Grandpa!

*(**GORDON** arrests his turn and faces **GORDIE**. **DONALD** turns toward **GORDIE**.)*

GORDON. That's great, Gee.

DONALD. Hello, Gordie.

*(The two men look at each other, a little smile erupts on each face, and each starts a gentle laugh. **GORDIE***

stands stationary, not understanding but happy, as simultaneously:)

– (All action freezes. The lights dim on all but **GORDIE,** *who is spotlighted, holding the model aircraft aloft.)*

– (Very Lynn's voice is heard singing "I'll see you again…")

(THE CURTAIN FALLS)

CLOSURE
was selected as the winner of the 2008 Samuel French Canadian Playwrights Contest. Samuel French established the Canadian Playwrights Contest to encourage awareness and growth of Canadian playwriting.

Past Samuel French Canadian Playwrights Contest winners include:

SHADOWS ON OAK ISLAND
by Garnet Hirst with Deborah L. Preeper

$38,000 FOR A FRIENDLY FACE
by Kristin Shepherd

BINGO BABES
by Isabel Duarte

KITCHEN WITCHES
by Caroline Smith

MAPLE LODGE
by Colleen Curran

THAT DARN PLOT
by David Belke

YEAR IN THE DEATH OF EDDIE JESTER
by T. Gregory Argall

For more about the these titles and the Canadian Playwrights Contest, visit samuelfrench.com

OTHER TITLES AVAILABLE FROM SAMUEL FRENCH

MAURITIUS
Theresa Rebeck

Comedy / 3m, 2f / Interior

Stamp collecting is far more risky than you think. After their mother's death, two estranged half-sisters discover a book of rare stamps that may include the crown jewel for collectors. One sister tries to collect on the windfall, while the other resists for sentimental reasons. In this gripping tale, a seemingly simple sale becomes dangerous when three seedy, high-stakes collectors enter the sisters' world, willing to do anything to claim the rare find as their own.

"(Theresa Rebeck's) belated Broadway bow, the only original play by a woman to have its debut on Broadway this fall."
- Robert Simonson, *New York Times*

"*Mauritius* caters efficiently to a hunger that Broadway hasn't been gratifying in recent years. That's the corkscrew-twist drama of suspense… she has strewn her script with a multitude of mysteries."
- Ben Brantley, *New York Times*

"Theresa Rebeck is a slick playwright… Her scenes have a crisp shape, her dialogue pops, her characters swagger through an array of showy emotion, and she knows how to give a plot a cunning twist."
- John Lahr, *The New Yorker*

Breinigsville, PA USA
02 November 2009
226815BV00002B/7/P